# Fly-Fishing-The Sacred Art

Casting A Fly As A Spiritual Practice
Rabbi Eric Eisenkramer
Rev. Michael Attas, MD
Foreword By Chris Wood, CEO, Trout
Unlimited
Preface By Lori Simon, Executive Director,
Casting For Recovery

EasyRead Large

# Copyright Page from the Original Book

**Library of Congress Cataloging-in-Publication Data**
Eisenkramer, Eric, 1975–
Fly-fishing—the sacred art : casting a fly as a spiritual practice / Rabbi Eric Eisenkramer and Rev. Michael Attas.
    p. cm.
Includes bibliographical references.
ISBN 978-1-59473-299-7 (pbk.)
1. Fly fishing. 2. Fishing—Religious aspects—Judaism. 3. Fishing—Religious aspects—Christianity. I. Attas, Michael, 1957- II. Title.
SH456.E39 2012
799.12'4—dc23
                            2012007106

10  9  8  7  6  5  4  3  2  1
Manufactured in the United States of America

Cover Design: Tim Holtz
Cover Photo ©iStockphoto.com/Douglas Allen, modified by Tim Holtz
Cover Art: "Greenback Cutthroat Trout" by James Prosek, in *Trout: An Illustrated History* (New York: Alfred A. Knopf, 1996), 103.

SkyLight Paths Publishing is creating a place where people of different spiritual traditions come together for challenge and inspiration, a place where we can help each other understand the mystery that lies at the heart of our existence.

SkyLight Paths sees both believers and seekers as a community that increasingly transcends traditional boundaries of religion and denomination——people wanting to learn from each other, *walking together, finding the way.*

SkyLight Paths, "Walking Together, Finding the Way," and colophon are trademarks of LongHill Partners, Inc., registered in the U.S. Patent and Trademark Office.

*Walking Together, Finding the Way®*
Published by SkyLight Paths Publishing
A Division of LongHill Partners, Inc.
Sunset Farm Offices, Route 4, P.O. Box 237
Woodstock, VT 05091
Tel: (802) 457-4000    Fax: (802) 457-4004
www.skylightpaths.com

# TABLE OF CONTENTS

# FOREWORD

Fly-fishing is dominated by two profound truths. First, anglers are optimists. Who other than an optimist would spend hours willingly—and joyfully—casting at river ghosts? An optimistic angler also knows that the last cast of the day will catch the day's largest fish. Second, anglers are a contemplative lot. Time spent in flowing water lends itself to serious thinking about spirituality, mortality, philosophy, and yes, even religion.

*Fly-Fishing—The Sacred Art: Casting a Fly as a Spiritual Practice* is a book about both of these truths. When I fish, I often find myself thinking about how I can be a better angler, parent, spouse, or friend. Depending on your level of faith, any angler can find solace or see the glory of the Divine in the wonder of a free-flowing river.

This book is not a paean to religion, do-gooders, deep ecology, or pantheism. Simultaneously, it is a combination of "Fly-Fishing 101" and "Reconnecting with Your Faith For Dummies." The messages from a Reform rabbi and an Episcopal priest are subtle, but hit home regardless of your faith or standing in the church. For example, in "In the Beginning," Reverend Mike likens fly-fishing to the Christian season of Advent:

*For me, preparing for a day on the river has an Advent feel to it. The annual Christian liturgical calendar begins with Advent, a time of preparation and hope. It is a time to hope—for new experiences on the waters we know and love. It is a time to dream—for new and wilder fish, new challenges, new waters to explore, new friends to fish with. It is a time to long for life on rivers that restores our souls and brings us back into harmony. In finding a small piece of the universe on the smallest of trout streams, we may learn our role in life and in the lives of those we love.*

In the book, Rabbi Eric describes serving as rabbi—literally meaning "teacher"—at the marriage ceremony of an expert angler, Bob, and Bob's betrothed, Marina. The Jewish marriage and faith traditions of standing under the *chuppah* (wedding canopy), the traditional blessings, and the breaking of glass all serve as a prelude to Bob and Eric becoming fishing buddies and learning from one another on the river.

Fly-fishing can seem intimidating to a novice, but Reverend Mike and Rabbi Eric do a great job of demystifying the sport by providing step-by-step instructions and helpful advice for beginners. Perhaps the most moving moments in the book are the small observations surrounding the intersection of life and fishing. In "Being There," Rabbi Eric talks about a common problem that new and expert anglers face: untangling a back-cast wrapped around a tree-branch.

*I am always trying to help people untangle complex situations in their lives: spiritual crises, difficult relationships with their loved ones, and other everyday challenges. I, too, have made mistakes that have created difficult knots: speaking harsh words in times of stress and anxiety, harming those I love with word and deed, and being too slow to forgive when hurt myself. As I work to untangle my fly, I remind myself that pulling too hard never works. But if I just try to fix my problems one step and one tangled loop at a time, there is the possibility of straightening them out and beginning anew.*

Likewise, Reverend Mike notes how as anglers and people we can sometimes get stuck in ruts. Often the best antidote is to try a new fly, river, approach, or attitude. In "Getting There," Reverend Mike writes:

*We like our lives packaged, comfortable, and familiar. Yet the Bible is full of stories of heroes called out of their comfort zone to take a journey. Giants of faith may argue, complain, whine, and groan, but finally they say, "Here I am Lord; send me." They are willing to risk everything in order to seek and follow.*

*Fishing is much like life in that regard. We can stay in our comfort zone, choosing flies we know and ways of thinking that we are comfortable with. But when we have the courage to open ourselves up to "newness," we are often rewarded with days where time is suspended and life is rediscovered.*

"Days where time is suspended, and life is rediscovered" is one of the finest distillations of why I fish. Fishing affirms my passion for life and provides an opportunity to reflect on my many blessings. Saint Augustine once asked, "For what is faith unless it is to believe what you do not see?" As anglers, we demonstrate that faith every time we cast our combinations of feathers, fur, and wire.

As the authors note in "Stewardship and Conservation," great fishing is not free. Population pressure, urbanization, and a myriad of other threats can compromise the places we love to fish. Great fishing occurs because people have made conscious decisions to donate their time or money to protect and restore natural habitats. Whether on Kettle Creek, a small river in Pennsylvania whose brook trout had been lost to pollution from coal mining but are now recovered; or a pristine landscape such as Bristol Bay that Trout Unlimited is working to protect from a proposed pebble mine, we need anglers to help give back to streams and rivers.

Whether you fish to experience the majesty of creation, or simply because you want to catch bigger trout, listen to Rabbi Eric and Reverend Mike. Get involved. Join Trout Unlimited. Teach a kid to fish. Clean up a river. Get out there.

—Chris Wood, CEO, Trout Unlimited

# PREFACE

As I began to read with delight *Fly-Fishing—The Sacred Art: Casting a Fly as a Spiritual Practice,* I was anticipating another "fish story" underscored with various musings on "this fishing practice" or "that casting method." What I found instead was a philosophy that exemplifies and parallels what those involved with Casting for Recovery feel at a cellular level and what one of our Montana Glacier retreat participants once expressed so well:

> *Fly-fishing is a 'be here now' activity. It takes focus, balance, and being centered, physically and emotionally, to stand in the river and cast. Living well after the diagnosis of breast cancer is best done in the moment as well. It takes focus, balance, and being centered to avoid feeling victimized by the diagnosis or anxious about any future recurrence. In both fly-fishing and living with breast cancer, the best that one can do is 'be here now' and hope.*

As over 70 percent of approximately seven hundred women who participate in a Casting for Recovery retreat each year have never attended a support group, their retreat weekend is often the first part of their journey, much like the journey to the river described in "In the Beginning," the opening chapter of *Fly-Fishing—The Sacred Art.* Many women do not know what to expect, have never been away from home alone, and their feelings of excitement meld with anxiety, fear, and anger—feelings that have become all too familiar since the day of their diagnosis.

The meditative exercises in *Fly-Fishing—The Sacred Art* are relevant to all as we meander along our own path in life. I am blessed to live in Battenkill Valley, New York, and drive along the river each day on my commute to work. One day, I found myself driving mindlessly to work, fretting about the day ahead. Death-gripping the steering wheel, late, and not in the present moment, I finally "came to" and forced myself to pull over. I got out of the car, stood stock-still, as if I were stalking trout, looked out toward the river, and gave thanks for the moment of reflection.

The final day of each Casting for Recovery retreat is a nondenominational spiritual gathering meant to further build a connection with each other and enhance the peace within ourselves. The text selections used in the retreat are drawn from many sources and traditions, both old and new. Just as Rabbi Eric and Reverend Mike provide us the opportunity for introspection and self-discovery, the same holds true for the Casting for Recovery retreat opportunity as is so wonderfully articulated in the following:

> *I have not missed the irony that something as insidious as breast cancer could give me*

*something so magical. I was walking around today thinking of you all and holding the specialness close. I never want to forget how I felt. I never want to forget the beautiful memories. I did not know what to expect but this was so much more than I imagined. The river is a symbol. Keep it with you.*

—Lori Simon, executive director, Casting for Recovery

# RABBI ERIC'S INTRODUCTION

*In my family, there was no clear division between religion and fly fishing.*

*—Norman Maclean (1902–1990), author,* A River Runs Through It

A century after Norman Maclean, the son of a Presbyterian minister, fished the Big Blackfoot River and found grace and beauty in casting a fly rod, and twenty years after Robert Redford released his lyrical film based on Maclean's novella, a rabbi and an Episcopal priest wade into the river of memory, story, and spirit.

I am a rabbi serving a congregation in Ridgefield, Connecticut—the Yankee Northeast. Born and raised in St. Louis, I have been on the East Coast for almost two decades, studying in Boston and New York City and serving congregations in Brooklyn and Long Island before taking my own pulpit in Connecticut.

Dr. Michael Attas is a cardiologist from Texas who, in his spare time, was ordained as an Episcopal priest and serves as a guest preacher at his local congregation. He is also a professor at Baylor University, where he teaches a class in medical humanities. While I am closer to the beginning of my rabbinical career, Mike is a seasoned pro in the hospital, the classroom, and the pulpit.

We are an unlikely pair, but Mike and I share something in common that transcends our different religions and backgrounds—a passion for fly-fishing. Mike has been a devoted angler for over forty years. During the summer months he not only casts his own flies but also works as a volunteer fly-fishing guide in Colorado. I got "hooked" on fly-fishing after I saw the film version of *A River Runs Through It* at the Hi-Pointe Theatre in St. Louis. For the last two decades, I have pursued trout of the Northeast from the storied rivers of the Catskills to the Housatonic and Farmington Rivers in my new home state of Connecticut. I also write about my angling adventures on the *Fly Fishing Rabbi,* a blog about trout, God, and religion.

A series of well-worn jokes begins: "A rabbi and a reverend walk into a bar..." Mike and I came together not for a drink, but rather to wade into the living waters that sustain trout as well as the watery depths of the spirit. We are a rabbi and a reverend who love to fish. Mike brings the teachings of Christianity to his experiences on the water. I find connections to Judaism each time I cast a fly in the trout stream. Norman Maclean saw no division between fly-fishing and religion. We believe that he was right. As clergy members of different faiths coming together to tell our stories, Mike and I believe that fly-fishing is a spiritual endeavor that can enrich our lives.

We begin the book with a trip to our home waters. These are the rivers whose riffles, pools, and runs we can see in our mind's eye and that we daydream about when driving to the grocery store or running errands. My home waters are the rivers of New York and Connecticut, streams that have brought anglers out of the big cities for centuries. Mike casts his flies to the trout of Colorado, leaving behind the flat plains of Texas for a few days in the tall mountains and the cold waters of the great American West.

We offer our stories separately—identified throughout the book as "Rabbi Eric: Stream and Spirit" and "Reverend Mike: Fishing into the Mystery." In the first half of this book, we describe a day fishing on our respective rivers. We begin with my story of fishing a favorite river near New York City, followed by a day on Mike's home waters in Colorado. Although separated by thousands of miles, our experiences on the stream run in parallel. Like anglers everywhere, we pack our gear; we leave our houses to head to our home on the river; we spend a day communing with the trout; and finally, we return to everyday life. It is a circular journey that cleanses our spirits and renews our souls.

While Mike and I love our home waters, after a while, it can all begin to feel too familiar. In the second half of this book, we leave the proverbial nest in search of new adventures. We share stories of fishing with family and friends—like my fishing buddy Bob and Mike's Zen-casting friend Candy—and recount our separate fishing trips in Argentina (once again showing how similarly the arc of our lives seems to flow).

In these pages we also explore two other aspects of fly-fishing—the creativity and artistry of tying flies and the importance of giving back to those rivers that we love through conservation and stewardship. At the end of each chapter we include reflection questions and exercises—some that focus on the skills of fly-fishing and others that seek to aid in spiritual awareness and growth.

For us, fly-fishing is about more than catching fish. We have been skunked—the angler's term for not catching anything—on the stream too many times to count, and stood shivering in our waders in 45-degree water long after sundown. Yet every chance we get, we head back to the river in search of trout and something more. It was Henry David Thoreau who said, "Many go fishing all their lives without knowing that it is not fish they are after."

We hope that this book will make you a better angler. In reading our stories you may begin to think differently about the time you spend on the stream and, as Thoreau suggested, pursue more than trout when wading into the river.

Fly-fishing helps Mike and I navigate the currents and eddies of our lives, draw closer to nature, and reflect upon our own inner journeys. Sometimes out on the water we even feel a presence larger than ourselves. We pause to look at the river, the trees, and the sky, and we simply say "thank you" for the amazing gifts of our world.

By sharing our journeys, Mike and I hope that you, too, will begin to fish with purpose and cast a fly with a new sense of meaning. Come join us as we explore together the potential for beauty, renewal, connection, and growth inherent in every trip to the stream.

# REVEREND MIKE'S INTRODUCTION

*I fish because I love to; because I love the environs where trout are found, which are invariably beautiful.... I thus escape, my fishing is at once an endless source of delight and an act of small rebellion; because I suspect that men are going along this way for the last time; only in the woods can I find solitude without loneliness.*

—*John D. Voelker (1903–1991), author,* Testament of a Fisherman

I have always seen my life in terms of landscape and journey. My earliest memories are of water, sky, mountains, and streams. I have been inspired by the natural world in ways that, even in my later stage of life, are both fulfilling and mystifying.

For one who was trained as a scientist, I see things in very mystical and weird ways. I look for meaning when it is elusive. I look for metaphor when my rational brain tells me that a rock is just a rock and a storm is just a storm. I search for and see trout in my sleep. I believe that time spent in nature exploring the wonders of fish and their habitat teaches us more about ourselves and our lives than we would ever learn otherwise. We find our humanity and wrestle with its dark side: fear, desire, failure, and weakness. And yet I've learned that when we let go and trust God, we are gifted with a memory of time that extends both back before we existed and forward to a time when our bodies no longer exist.

Like most of us, I am enchanted with the notion of journey. I have done my share of wonderful road trips, one or two of which I share with you in these pages. I love to explore, wander, dream, and engage creation on its own terms. The human spirit is always best expressed in terms of journey. We travel from desert to mountaintop and there we find the burning bush that is not consumed. We baptize in water—quite literally, we drown each other and emerge as new creatures, born again with hopes and dreams for a better way of relating to both our fellow humans and our precious earth.

In my life in medicine, I meet people in all stages of journeying. They are the walking, the broken, the wounded, and the glorious. When pressed, they all see their lives in terms of stages and growth—some fitful, some elusive, some traveling backward on paths that lead to treacherous ground, and some moving forward to redemption and hope. We are human, one and all. We all need language, symbols, and journeys to hang our hats upon as we seek to find ourselves, as well as the God who not only created us but—I believe—continues to love and care for us despite our futile attempts to go it alone.

Fishing captures and symbolizes the completeness of the human spirit and journey. I see each journey to the river as a tiny recapitulation of my own humanity and the things I share in common with my fellow travelers.

This book was born of our need to express how we experience spirituality in the cool, clear waters of trout streams. It is the product of a wonderful two-year journey with new friend, fellow angler, and coauthor Eric Eisenkramer, who has enchanted and gifted me with his words of faith from a tradition that I feel a part of in my very marrow. I hope and pray that my words may stand beside his, drawing each reader into the beauty and depth of our respective traditions. I have learned so much from him, and I have been fortunate to draw on his wisdom and love of his faith and of waters that we both share.

From these pages we hope you find your own delight in water and journey. Early in my fly-fishing career I remember telling a friend that there is so much to learn! Some forty years later, that is still true. Every trip I learn something new about rivers, fish, and the natural world. Most importantly, I learn something new about myself. Every encounter with the waters of our planet draws me deeper into who I am and who I want to become.

Whatever your religious tradition may be, our hope is that these words may draw you deeper into yourself, God, one another, and our beloved creation. We have offered suggestions that draw upon our own traditions and experiences. We also trust that they may be starting points for your journey that emerges from your own heritage as you search for God in waters that are holy for us all. If they succeed at any level, then we have received the greater gift.

# CHAPTER ONE

# IN THE BEGINNING

## PREPARING FOR THE RIVER

*The charm of fishing is that it is the pursuit of what is elusive but attainable, a perpetual series of occasions for hope.*

*—John Buchan (1875–1940), novelist, historian, and politician*

# RABBI ERIC: STREAM AND SPIRIT

It is 10:00a.m., the first Monday in April, and my favorite fly-fishing rod is broken.

Opening Day for trout fishing in New York is April 1, but this year that falls on a Saturday, the Jewish Sabbath. As a Jew, that means no fishing. Nor could I make it to the stream on Sunday. As a rabbi, I am busy teaching.

So my first chance to cast a fly after the long winter was delayed for two excruciating days. All through the state, from the famous Beaverkill River in the Catskills to the Salmon River in the north, my fellow anglers had two glorious days out on the stream ahead of me.

Monday morning, April 3, I grab my fishing bag out of the trunk and bring it to the porch to prepare for a trip to the Connetquot River on Long Island. All of my fly gear lives in an old green duffle bag in the trunk of my car. There is something reassuring about having my fishing gear close, because it means that I could head to the stream at a moment's notice. I never want to be too far away from my fly rod.

When I unzip the duffle, the smell of the stream rises into the air. It is an unmistakable scent; one of water, plants, and fish. It smells of life. They say that of the five senses, smell has the strongest connection to memory. When I open my fly-fishing bag and smell the stream, the bends and turns of the Connetquot appear in my mind's eye.

Everything comes out of the bag—waders, boots, wading staff, vest, and flies—to be surveyed and checked. The waders do not have any new leaks, even though on previous trips I hiked through a maze of thorns. A bit of wax applied to the wading staff ensures that it will come apart easily for storage.

Out come the fly boxes. The brown and rainbow trout of the Connetquot go crazy for the Elk Hair Caddis, attacking the dry-fly pattern with loud thumps on the surface of the stream. I make sure to have at least a half dozen in brown and black. For the middle of the day, when the sun covers the river and trout are unlikely to rise, the subsurface nymphs are the most effective, especially the Copper John with a red or brown metal coil body. For this trip, I make sure to have an assortment of other choices: Griffith's Gnats, Adams Flies, ants, beetles, and Woolly Buggers and nymphs in green, black, and brown.

Almost as an afterthought, I decide to put together my fly rod and take a few casts on the lawn to refresh my muscle memory and get the feel of the line in my fingers.

I put together the four parts of my fifteen-year-old St. Croix 5/6-weight rod, a warhorse that I purchased in my hometown of St. Louis when I first realized that you could cast to a trout without a worm.

I grab the reel and slip it into its place on the rod as I have done dozens of times before, only to discover that the reel seat is broken, that the metal latch that holds the reel in place spins freely around. An intense heat of frustration spreads from my chest as I realize that my first day of fishing in months might be over before it even starts. My head begins to spin like the fly reel that will not stay put on the rod.

Twenty minutes later I am standing in the "adhesives" aisle of a large, chain hardware store, holding one-quarter of a fly rod before a man with a neon-orange vest and a nametag that reads "Bill." Will Bill be my salvation, finding a way to glue together a fishing rod and, in doing so, reattach my hopes of a day of glorious trout on the stream? He sends me home with a two-color epoxy, one tube of white and one of black. When you combine the two, he says, it will form a strong paste that will seal the reel for a hundred years.

Being a rabbi, I had already endowed this humble two-tone glue with all sorts of symbolism: the black and white representing the good and evil inclinations within us all that blend together to form our humanity. Or I figured that the black-and-white glues were like the yin and yang, opposites that complement one another and form harmony. But when I get home and push the plunger to blend the two glues, they form a dull gray paste. I spread some of the glue on the reel seat. It is an ugly repair, a glop of gray epoxy on an otherwise beautiful, brown, sleek fiberglass rod. But it will have to do.

By now it is noon, and if I'm going to make it the fifty miles from my home in Queens to the stream, I have to get going. This day of fishing will be either an unmitigated disaster or a great save. Only time will tell.

Every trip to the river begins with a hike a few blocks uphill to my car, with my green duffle and fly rod in tow. I refuse to pay the $200 a month to park my Honda Civic in the garage of my building in Queens, since there are free spaces on the street. I used to pull the car around to the front of the building and double-park to load my fishing gear. But the time that

I found a $150 ticket on my windshield from the always-roving New York City parking police put an end to that.

With gear secured, I start the car. The trip from Forest Hills to the Connetquot River on the south shore of Long Island takes an hour. With the windows down, the cool April air flows in between the seats. The New York City apartment buildings and duplexes stacked side by side begin to give way to a suburban landscape of trees, grass, and family homes. As I speed down the road with the other cars, I wonder if, from above, we look like trout in the stream, lined up and swimming down the highway.

As I drive toward the river, I think about another trip that I made last week, only on that drive I did not want to reach my destination, a cemetery in Brookfield, Connecticut, where I was to officiate at the funeral of Larry S.

As I drove up a small road, I saw the sign—United Jewish Center Cemetery—set a ways back. I was reminded of how anti-Semitism has shaped Jewish architecture: synagogues have no Jewish symbols on their facades and are pushed back well off the street to be less conspicuous. This cemetery has a sign hidden back in the trees of Connecticut.

I parked the car and went to visit the family. When I spotted Larry's daughter, I understood fully why I did not want to be there. Emily is a tall twelve-year-old with glasses and a sweet smile, and she had just lost her father.

As I delivered the eulogy I had prepared, it got harder and harder to speak. Larry loved the outdoors, especially when he was out in nature with his daughter. They went hiking and fishing together, staying out past dusk even in the winter.

The sadness rose in my body, and I had to pause before concluding. Then I said: "This cemetery is near one of Larry and Emily's favorite trails. Larry will find his eternal rest near the nature that he loved to share with his daughter."

As I read that line, Larry S. was suddenly my father, too, whose name is also Larry. When I was twelve years old, my dad took me hiking and fishing on the bass lakes of Missouri every summer. We watched the red-and-white bobber float on the lake and talked together. And then I realized that I, too, was Larry S. In a few years I will be taking my twin son and daughter hiking in Pierrepont State Park and fishing on the trout streams of Connecticut. After the eulogy, we all recited the Jewish mourner's prayer, the *Kaddish,* for Larry. The family and friends went to shovel a pile of dirt into the grave, participating in the burial as is Jewish tradition. I got in line as well, as that day I was a mourner too.

Whether I wake up to discover a broken fly rod or that all of my gear is prepared and packed, whether the drive on New York City highways is quick or I am mired in traffic, whether I watch the cars zip by like trout in the stream or get lost in my own thoughts of life and death and memories, no trip to the river is without the potential for reflection. Rather than seeing the drive to the stream as wasted time, it can be a prelude to a day of fishing, a time to let go of the everyday and begin to look within.

# REVEREND MIKE: FISHING INTO THE MYSTERY

It begins with a quickening of the pulse, a combination of haste and anticipation that hasn't lessened in over thirty-five years. It is not a cognitive experience at all, but something that happens on a deeper, existential level. While there are many thoughts that go through my mind as I prepare to fish my favorite river, the Frying Pan River in western Colorado, they begin as sensations in my body rather than a checklist in my brain.

Experience begins in the heart and soul, deep places of longing and desire. In a sense, a trip to the river is sort of a cosmic journey to the heart of our human connection to the earth, to the Divine, and to all of creation. But ultimately dreams give way to reality, so that is where we must begin.

Since I travel to the Frying Pan multiple times a year, it is inevitable that I keep my gear ready to grab at a moment's notice. A corner of my garage is home to the mélange of loaded rods, waders, boots, fly vests, and fishing hats. While I have a system to keep chaos at bay, it is not perfect. I have been known to forget essentials such as wading boots, or the correct fly box for the season, or (my concession to aging) a good pair of magnifiers that are all too necessary to tie on a tiny, size 24 midge in the middle of the river on a cold, windy day.

This morning, I stare at the tepee of rods I stow in what looks like an oversized pipe rack, their various lengths, colors, and diameters a thicket of mismatched sticks. It takes a while, this staring thing, because choosing what rods to take with me is one of the most important decisions I have to make each time I head to the river.

The Frying Pan can require anything from a 1-weight for little brookies in the tributary creeks, to a strong 6-weight when the water is high on the main stem, and the current and wind are stiff. My normal rod for all-purpose use is a lovely, delicate 3-weight that casts like a dream and sets a tiny dry fly down like a feather. I am no purist—I will nymph when the conditions are right—but I prefer casting to rising fish with dry flies. Therefore, I tend to use soft-tip rods, 7X tippet, and an old fashioned, burnished copper, Hardy reel. All my favorite gear is well worn and aged like its owner. Over the years it has absorbed the life of the river, a life I feel the minute I curve my hand to the rod grip.

I am sure that choosing a rod may seem like a technical feat in and of itself when you are new to the sport, but the mystery of new terminology is built upon a nice symmetry of principles.

The primary difference between fly-fishing and spin casting is that, in fly-fishing, you cast the line, and in spin or bait casting, you cast the bait or artificial lure. In other words, the weight of the fly line throws the fly, as opposed to the weight of the lure throwing the line. It is nothing more than the difference between Newtonian physics and quantum physics: one is simple mechanics, and one is a movement of eternity. By writing that, I realize I am tipping my hat about my preferences!

A fly line is assigned a numerical value by a rather precise measurement of its weight. A 1-weight line is the smallest, lightest line manufacturers make. It would typically be used for small wild fish, like brook trout, small panfish, and so on. A 12- to 13-weight line would be a very heavy line designed for large saltwater gamefish, like tarpon, marlin, and others. Rods are then matched to the weight of the line.

While most people will normally choose, for example, a 5-weight rod to cast a 5-weight line, I often prefer to "overweight" a rod so that it loads more quickly and efficiently. Overweighting is a matter of choosing a line slightly heavier than the rod designation calls for. In the right situations, it helps a rod take advantage of the loading phenomenon where the line weight is used to put an appropriate flex on the rod on the backcast, then is propelled forward on the forward cast to lay the line out delicately and straight. I have found that slightly "overweighting" a rod may help it load better in wind or tight fishing quarters—not mandatory, so much as a personal quirk.

After I choose the rod I'll use for the day, there are more decisions to be made before I get on the road, and the next is one of my favorites.

When confronted, most fly-fishers will admit to some slightly superstitious behavior they indulge in when preparing to fish. Mine has to do with hats. I have several dozen fishing hats, some with better karma than others. The good karma hats have caught more fish, seen more joy and heartbreak, and experienced more glory than others. Each has its own history. I relish them, because they connect me to my past as well as my hopes for the future.

Often I will take three to four hats to the river, and, depending on some mysterious vibe, choose the right hat for the day. I take my time with this ritual, because there is nothing worse than getting in the water and finding I have chosen the wrong hat. But I am also of the belief that an unlucky hat one day can be fortuitous the next. I am willing to give some of the lower-ranked hats a second chance ... even a third. Like life, we can always experience rebirth, even in something so seemingly trivial as the choice of a hat.

My favorite is an old, faded, orange Sage hat. It has witnessed the catching of thousands of fish and absorbed the smell of rivers, cigar smoke, sweat, tears, and laughter. I wore it when I went to Argentina to fish and grieve after the loss of a dear friend. I wore it when I flew to the river after my mother's funeral, and it protected me stoically as I fished through rivers of tears. I love its feel, its character, and its quiet, worn strength. It seems to have wisdom, and I trust it to comfort me through hard times and accompany me through good times.

While this may be nothing more than one more of those fishing superstitions that we all are given to, the gear I choose for the day often mirrors my inner soul and space. When I am centered and mellow, I seem to gravitate toward the old and faded Sage hat. When I am stressed, I often choose a hat from Saint Benedicts Monastery in Snowmass, home of the well-known Trappist monk, Thomas Keating. Perhaps I unconsciously hope that the good karma of that place will flow from my hat into my hands and the water. If I have been playing golf and had a particularly good round and felt a swing freedom and tempo that "worked," I will take that same golf hat to the river, hoping its magic is transferable.

Shirts and vests are subject to the same mystery. I have a few old favorites, typically soft colors to blend with the soft light of our rivers here. Many of them are frayed, worn, and have tiny holes where flies have pierced the fabric. But they feel "right," and therefore are part of my identity on the water. I prefer shirts, vests, and jackets with lots of pockets. I need room for cigars, extra glasses, and the various and sundry doodads that all anglers tend to collect.

Most of us tend to have a pack-rat mentality, and while it may look to an outsider to be a mess, it is really loosely organized chaos. At least that's how I would describe my gear on a given day.

I have learned the hard way to carry my fishing license in my shirt pocket. One day I was in the middle of a major green-drake hatch in my favorite part of the river. It was reasonably crowded, so finding a good run to work by myself was no easy chore to start with.

A very nice game warden walked along the bank, smiling sweetly as she watched me land fish after fish, then gently motioned with her index finger and asked for my license. I smiled back and said that the fish were rising like crazy and my license was in the car. Would she mind waiting a bit more while the hatch continued? She continued to smile and shook her head no.

So I trudged remorsefully out of the river, crossing a deep riffle that took some time, walked with her up to the car, and showed her my valid and up-to-date license. I even shared a bottle of cold water with her, as she clearly had been out working all afternoon. She could not have been nicer, and, despite my frustrations, I knew she was right and only doing her job. By the time I managed to navigate my way back to my slot, the hatch was almost over. So be it. Lesson learned.

A person can never have too much gear for all the various scenarios that might be encountered in this Colorado valley. Mountain storms can appear without warning, so I have learned to be prepared for them. I take rain gear on the sunniest of days, windbreakers, layers, and fishing gloves and winter parkas for the winter months. I have seen days in May or June when I've fished in a driving snowstorm in the morning followed by sun and short-sleeved weather in the afternoon. What is interesting is that the best fishing is always in the middle of the worst weather—as if we are rewarded for our fortitude and courage.

One of the things I love most about fly-fishing is the way it can take where I "am" and allow me not only to live fully in the moment, but often to transform it into something new and even better. To do that with honesty and authenticity requires something that spiritual giants are always writing about—and that is the ability to look honestly inward. Thomas Merton knew that any honest journey outward to the world always begins with the journey inward. He titled one of his books *Contemplation in a World of Action*—the title itself offering a very telling insight into human nature and our relationship with others as well as the Divine.

So often we fear looking honestly at our moods, our souls, our fears, our hopes, and our dreams for unity. We use false masks to protect us from the world, its dangers, and the unknown shadow sides of ourselves. So, for me, an honest trip to the river begins with a self-assessment.

What sort of mood am I in? Are there frustrations with work, life, relationships, or time management that are gently fraying at the edges of my soul? Or am I more or less centered and mellow? Do I feel rushed and out of rhythm with myself? If so, I am certain to take those issues to the river, and the negativity of them will affect my peace there ... and usually the fishing, as well. I seem to fish with more grace and freedom when I'm honest about my feelings and issues.

For me, preparing for a day on the river has an Advent feel to it. The annual Christian liturgical calendar begins with Advent, a time of preparation. It is a time to hope—for new experiences on the waters we know and love. It is a time to dream—for new and wilder fish, new challenges, new waters to explore, new friends to fish with. It is a time to long for life on rivers that restores our souls and brings us back into harmony. In finding a small piece of the universe on the smallest of trout streams, we may learn our role in life and in the lives of those we love.

# The Fly-Angler's Gear Checklist

**Fly-fishing rods:** 7- to 9-foot graphite rods are used on most trout streams. Some anglers also fish with split cane bamboo rods that they construct themselves.

**Reels:** Designed to match the line weight, the reel holds the fly line and creates drag necessary to reel in the fish.

**Fly Lines:** 5- to 7-weight lines are most often used for trout with a choice of floating line or sinking line for fishing deeper waters. The bright fluorescent color is for the benefit of the angler and is not seen by the fish.

**Leaders and tippets:** The clear, tapered leader, 7 1/2- to 9-feet long, is tied to the end of the fluorescent fly line. Next comes a length of an even thinner tippet, with the fly tied to the end.

**Flies:** Trout flies come in even-numbered sizes, 10 through 24, based on the size of the hook used to tie the fly; the larger the number, the smaller the fly. Dry flies are fished on the surface of the stream, nymphs and streamers sink into the river. Many anglers push down the barb on the hook to make it easier to release the trout back into the river unharmed.

**Waders, boots, and wading staff:** Waders are made of neoprene or rubber. Wading boots come with felt soles or rubber soles with metal studs. The latter have become more popular in recent times as they prevent the spread of invasive species in rivers. A metal wading staff helps the angler keep balance in larger and faster moving streams.

**Other Essentials**
Fishing license

Net

Vest

Forceps (to remove the hook from the mouth of the fish)

Fly boxes, fly float for dry flies, split-shot weights, and strike indicators for nymphs

**Other Good Stuff to Have**
Notebook and pen

Bug spray

Sunscreen

Flashlight

Water and snacks

Cell phone (in case of emergency)

## Reflection Questions

1.  What are your favorite parts of preparing for a day of fly-fishing? What other journeys in life require spiritual or emotional preparation? How

can we ready our minds and souls for the good and bad, the difficult and rewarding, that we all can encounter?

2. What are some items of fishing gear or clothing that have special significance to you? What do these objects remind you of, and why are they meaningful to you?

3. Like a fly-fishing rod or vest, our faith traditions also require gear such as a cross worn around a person's neck or a tallis, the Jewish ritual prayer shawl. How can spiritual gear aid you in your life? Think about a time when your spiritual gear has especially supported you in a time of personal challenge.

## Exercise: The Significance of Your Gear

When preparing for your next fishing trip, take a few moments to think about your fly-fishing gear. Choose one or two items that have personal significance, that remind you of special times spent on your home waters or on trips to distant rivers. Jot down these memories or stories about your favorite fishing rod or hat and tuck them into a plastic bag or waterproof pocket of your vest. Now, as you prepare to head to the stream, each item of your gear will take on a new and deeper meaning.

# CHAPTER TWO

# GETTING THERE

## ESCAPING THE EVERYDAY

*Fishing is not an escape from life, but often a deeper immersion into it.*

*—Harry Middleton (1949–1993), American nature writer*

# REVEREND MIKE: FISHING INTO THE MYSTERY

I pull out of the driveway in Colorado and catch a gravel road that bends to the southwest. Immediately to my left is Mount Sopris—the holy mountain of the Ute Indians who wintered in this valley. Invariably, it takes my breath away. The hues of verdant green, yellow, orange, and purple sage change with the seasons. Sopris itself towers above the valley floor like a crown jewel. It has a softness and quiet strength about it that brings me to some deep, still place as I begin the journey to the Frying Pan River. At dawn, it always feels as if God shines a beacon of holy light on the peak, striking it before the rest of the valley lights up with the birth of a new day.

There is something to be said about the familiarity of place. Both the inner landscape of our spiritual lives and the rivers we fish often come to symbolize our comfort zones. They are like wrapping up in a familiar, soft, warm blanket, with smells coming from the kitchen of fresh-brewed coffee and your favorite breakfast casserole cooling on the table.

When fishing home waters, it is reassuring to see familiar rocks, riffles, and pools. I know them as well as I know my own strengths and weaknesses. I know the way fish hold in certain patterns and at certain times of day. I know the way light moves through the canyon in different seasons, and the way storm clouds can blow through without warning and change the waters in a heartbeat. I know the way water levels fluctuate, and how this affects the fish and insect life cycles. Knowing these things helps to ground me, keeping me rooted in my inner self. When the magic happens, I know how to simply get out of the way and immerse myself in the moment. My brain can go on autopilot, and the mystery of the waters takes me away.

At the bottom of a steep hill, I catch one more view of Sopris to the south before taking Colorado Route 82 heading east into Basalt. I often stop at Taylor Creek Fly Shop to chat with my friends there, pick up any flies that I might be missing, and look at water flows for the day.

As I pull into the familiar parking lot outside of the shop, I begin to feel truly alive and at home. I have fished in many waters and stopped at many fly shops, but the men who have worked here are as genuine and as kind to anglers as anyone could ever hope to meet. Their knowledge and love of the water is contagious, and there is nothing they like more than sharing stories or current stream information. Sure, I could head up and get started on my own. But the ritual of conversation with trusted friends is part of the journey.

Tim, the store manager, has been in the valley for decades. I didn't know him in his early years, but, from the stories, I gather he was a fun-loving, world-class guide in his own right. I suspect the true old-timers in the Roaring Fork valley would have more than a few stories to share about him. His knowledge of insect life, fish, and water is simply astounding. Just when I begin to feel I finally have mastered some of the nuances of this river system, a conversation with Tim is all I need to remind me of my own limitations, which is a good thing!

And what is most astounding is his generosity of spirit, his sharing of a pure, unadulterated love of the sport. Men like him freely bequeath their gifts to the future, and knowing him is just one more example of the grace-filled moments that imbue an angler's life.

Kirk, one of the other men who works there, is the one who came up to my house one winter after I had major ankle surgery to give me my first fly-tying lessons. I was in a funk and feeling sorry for myself, as my family was going to the mountain to ski without me for the first time ever. That time with Kirk was healing for mind and soul, and I began to understand the beauty and delicacy of the art that goes into a well-tied fly.

My surgical background has made the "technical moves" with my fingers fairly easy, but it was Kirk who helped me make the leap from a live fly in a certain stage of its life in moving water to a different kind of life emerging from the jaws of my fly-tying vise.

Finally, there is Will, who works the desk and guides, and who is a wonderful, interesting, and gifted soul. He and the others helped my wife choose flies from the valley in different stages of their life cycle and had them mounted with brass nameplates in a huge shadow box that hangs in my study. It is always amazing to watch the eyes of guests who have no knowledge of fly-fishing when they see the diversity and size of bugs that will catch fish in this valley!

The Frying Pan flow rates vary between 100 cubic feet per second (cfs) and as high as 900-plus, depending on the snowpack and water needs downstream. I have found the fishing best between 200 and 300 cfs, but I have fished on the sides when the river is very high and waded the whole thing in very low conditions. The fish are always there—they don't migrate.

The river has very predictable insect cycles, so it is easy to be prepared for either a *dry* fly or a *nymph* version of the fly appropriate for the season. A dry fly is an imitation of a flying insect that has hatched and flies around, landing on the water. When a trout is keyed in on this stage, they will either sip or voraciously inhale a dry pattern that matches what is naturally in the air. If there are no bugs either in the air or visible on the surface, one needs to fish with a nymph pattern, which is simply an artificial imitation of a pupa stage that has hatched from eggs in the gravel of the river bottom and is swimming towards the surface. Often fish will key in on this stage when there are no flying insects visible. At times, I will choose a dry-dropper technique where the first fly is a dry pattern of the hatch. I also suspend a nymph of the same insect 16–18 inches below the dry. Once I get a feel for what the fish are feeding on, I usually use two varieties of the same life cycle in slightly different colors or sizes.

This river is a year-round fishery, with no "season" per se. The season is whenever you get there and have the proper mind set to let the waters begin their healing magic. In the spring there are lovely little blue winged olives (BWOs) in abundance. Early summer brings out the famous caddis hatch, which is referred to colloquially as the "Mother's Day caddis hatch." People come from all over the world to experience the mid- to late-summer western mayfly hatches: pale morning duns (PMDs) and green drakes. The green drakes are migratory, so when they arrive in Basalt from their journey beginning on the Colorado River in Glenwood Springs, we know it'll be a week or two before they work their way up the Frying Pan. That's when the party begins. The trout get in a feeding frenzy, giving us anglers six to eight weeks of the finest dry fly-fishing in the world.

Finally, the drakes and PMDs begin to die off, and the fall gives way to blue-winged olives again, followed by the tiny midge fishing of the winter season. It is all good and delightful in its own way.

One of the things that I always enjoy about stopping at Taylor Creek Fly Shop is talking to the guys about new or interesting flies that are "hot." Between the flies I tie on my own and the more technical and difficult ones, I normally have a fairly good selection to get me through most days. But I'm always amazed to see the nuances to standard flies that people can come up with. It is a testament to human creativity to see how the human mind can step outside of its "boxes" to solve old problems in new and diverse ways.

I love to see imagination at work, and interesting flies always spark my creative juices. In my mind's eye, I see the fish watching these new patterns and saying to themselves, "that looks like something I might like today!" The fish in the Frying Pan get heavy fishing pressure, and anglers tend to get locked into the same way of thinking about choosing a fly that they have heard about. Often a fish will get excited about a familiar pattern that has the tiniest bit of unusual difference.

Perhaps I am anthropomorphizing, but fish often behave just like we do. We like our lives packaged, comfortable, and familiar. Yet the Bible is full of stories of heroes called out of their comfort zone to take a journey. Giants of faith may argue, complain, whine, and groan, but finally they say, "Here I am Lord; send me." They are willing to risk everything in order to seek and follow.

Fishing is much like life in that regard. We can stay in our comfort zone, choosing flies we know and ways of thinking that we are comfortable with. But when we have the courage to open ourselves up to "newness," we are often rewarded with days where time is suspended and life is rediscovered.

I leave the fly shop to cover the final distance to the Frying Pan, the meandering thirteen mile tailwater fishery that is legendary for numbers and quality of trout. As I said, it gets very heavy fishing pressure year round, but I've spent thousands of hours there, and I know not only the popular places but the hidden treasures.

Since the Frying Pan is a "tailwater" river, it flows from its beginnings in Reudi Reservoir at a fairly constant temperature of 39°F–41°F year-round. So, if you fish on a warm summer day the water is still fairly cold; if you fish in the dead of winter and the air temperature is 10°F the water feels downright balmy! Our senses deceive us, yet the river is always doing its thing no matter what we puny humans bring to the journey.

The fish on the Frying Pan are the classic western trout—predominantly browns and rainbows. We have a rare brook trout and cutthroat on the upper river, as well as a hybrid of cutthroat and rainbow trout called a "cutbow." Parts of the river are stocked and will often get the heaviest fishing pressure, yet there are plenty of wild trout that will live their lives within a few hundred yards of their spawning ground.

In our section of the country, the browns spawn in the winter and the rainbows in the spring. I love to gently wade the spawning areas in those months, treading lightly around the actual beds where I see spawning activity. At times I will not even take a rod, but take instead my large, bulky Nikon camera, hoping to capture moments of beauty, grace, and rebirth.

I love being in the water in those times, feeling the air that tastes so sweet and the wind that comes from the heavens. I have been known to find a rock or a grassy bank and just be still, soaking it all in and letting the cares of the world seep out from my body. I love the wild birds that inhabit our waters—eagles, hawks, bluebirds, lovely yellow warblers, Canada geese, and ducks. They soar above our river and nest on its banks. Once again, they bring me home in my soul to places I need to go, over and over.

Christians have a very radical and often misunderstood notion of how God and Jesus are connected to the human condition. Called the incarnation, it is simply the idea that God poured himself into humanity through the bodily person of Jesus of Nazareth. The "word became flesh": God incarnated himself in order to bring humanity back home.

But there is a little known variation of this that has been discussed by more radical theologians called "panentheism." It is quite different from polytheism, which basically states that there are innumerable gods. Instead, panentheism makes the claim that God is in all matter and all of creation. All humans have this spark of divinity within us, as does all of matter—earth, waters, fish, birds, forests, and trees.

I sense this on the water time after time. I sense not separateness from God but union. I sense not distance from water but a merger. My life energy is joined with the life that surrounds me each and every time I wade into the waters. We are incarnated fragments of God, one and all.

We all have our issues that suck at the marrow of our soul. But fishing brings me face-to-face not only with my weakness, but with my strength. I experience living, breathing, radical life-giving God in each and every wisp of wind, riffle, deer sighting, and shimmer of flashing trout.

# RABBI ERIC: STREAM AND SPIRIT

By the time I pull up to the front gate of Connetquot State Park, the only things on my mind are how soon I can be on the river and if the large trout will be rising.

The shack at the park entrance looks like the world's tiniest drive-through restaurant. It is a squat, square building with sliding windows on each side. The park warden opens the window, and, rather than handing me a sack of burgers and fries, she holds out a clipboard.

The Connetquot River runs on a "beat" system, which is similar, I am told, to the way the British fish the great chalk streams of England, like the Itchen and the Test. At the Connetquot, it is a two-step process: first you sign in at the shack, which only gets you a place in line; then you must return at 4:30p.m. sharp, wait for your name to be called, and select the beat you would like on the stream. You had better be on time because, by 4:45 the spots are divvied up, and by 5:00 the shack is empty. Only in New York does it take this much effort to go fishing.

Today I am third on the list to select a beat. It's a little disappointing, because I always like to be first in line for the important things in life, like fishing and jazz. For the yearly jazz concert in college, I would arrive at the box office at 7:00a.m. to have my pick of seats. That was especially important the year I took my then girlfriend (and now wife) on a date to see Wynton Marsalis. Today, I'm not sure if third in line will be good enough to get one of the coveted middle beats, but we'll have to see.

I drive past the shack and park the car in the small gravel lot. It is a little after 1:00p.m., and I have a few hours to wait. I leave my green duffle in the car so I can hike unencumbered into the park. As I walk away from the car, I pass by a small wooden post with a sign on it that tells me I am standing on the old Native American road, exactly 50 miles from New York City. It might as well have been 500 miles, as pavement has given way to dirt, tall buildings to large trees.

A few more steps and I stand before a large, old, three-story house with dark, wooden shingles and green, painted window trim that overlooks an oval lake. Built in 1820 as Snedecor's Tavern, this was the clubhouse of the South Side Sportsmen's Club of Long Island for over one hundred years, before being bought by New York State. I am fishing the same stream where anglers have cast a fly for close to two centuries, and where Native Americans fished long before that.

The tiny gift shop is open, and I purchase a Connetquot River T-shirt decorated with three silk-screened bright red and orange flies. I like to have a memento of every stream I fish: a T-shirt or metal button for my vest from the well-known stream, or some small, natural artifact. When fishing the Rio Quines, a trout stream in rural Argentina, I grabbed one of the metallic pieces of mica that were strewn all around the river. The thin, gray rock glistened in the sun like the side of a rainbow trout. I put it in my pocket to remember that day.

There is a dilapidated, wooden bench in front of the clubhouse facing the lake that has probably been there for a few decades. The hard wood is not very comfortable, but I sit down anyway. I see the lake stretching before me, a quarter mile wide and half mile long. The river feeds the lake from the north, and a dam sits at the southern edge. Downstream of the dam, the tidal river flows on to the Atlantic Ocean.

A half dozen Canada geese float near the opposite shore, along with a pair of large, white swans with graceful, arched necks. Today, the sun is shining brightly in the blue April sky. The water is calm and cool. As I sit on my wooden perch, I survey the lake and listen to the sound of the wind. I feel my shoulders drop, the tension that resides there six days a week beginning to ease. I stop moving and thinking, and just live, breathing and existing, at one with all that surrounds me. Sitting on the bench in front of the lake, it feels like the Sabbath.

Twentieth-century Jewish philosopher Rabbi Abraham Joshua Heschel calls the Sabbath "a palace in time." Six days a week we seek to create in the realm of space, wrestling with the world and seeking profit from the earth. On the Sabbath we let go of the everyday in order to focus on existence and eternity. We pray, we study, we spend time with loved ones, we eat, we live, we rest. The palace of the Sabbath is like a fortress, a welcome day of respite from the challenges of existence.

On Friday night and Saturday I celebrate Shabbat, the Jewish Sabbath, praying and studying with my congregation. But in the spring and summer, Monday is my fly-fishing Sabbath, when I take time to stretch out on a wooden bench in front of the lake, and I watch the swans, feel the breeze, and know that I, too, am part of the eternal cycle of the earth.

After a few minutes of soaking in this fly-fishing Sabbath, sitting on the hard bench makes my back start to hurt, and almost as quickly I get bored. Moments of holiness always seem to be so fleeting. It's time to find something else to do.

I walk past the lake, upstream through the woods, until I arrive at the trout hatchery. The flow of the Connetquot here is divided into three long rectangular concrete pools, one for each of the three trout species that swim in the rivers of the Northeast.

The smallest of the three, the brook trout, is distinguished by light spots on dark skin and white-edged fins. Brookies are native to the Northeast and favor small, cold streams. Rainbow trout evolved in the rivers of the Pacific Coast, from Alaska to Mexico, and now reside in waters throughout the world. Named for their brilliant colors of silver, pink, and green, 'bows can grow quite large. The workhorses of most northeastern streams are the brown trout, hearty fish that can tolerate less-than-ideal stream conditions. "Brownies" are native to Europe and come in shades of green and brown with dark spots.

Standing before the rainbow trout pool, I see hundreds of trout backs, packed in like riders on the New York City subway that I gladly left behind this morning. I drop my quarter in the slot of a red gumball machine, and, cupping my hand beneath the opening, I pull open the small metal door. Instead of the usual small pink ball of gum, the machine spits out a few dozen tiny brown pellets—trout food. I wonder if this artificial trout food is any healthier for the fish than the gumball would be for me.

I walk to the edge of the pool, toss a few pellets in, and the water comes to life in a violent maelstrom, the trout literally jumping over one another to get the brown corn treats. Trout are aggressive hunters and will attack a mayfly on the surface of a stream with a loud thump. But stick dozens of trout in a hatchery pool, and the fight for food is amplified. My fishing buddy Bob said that you can always tell a hatchery trout by its rounded fins, which were made dull by the constant rubbing against the concrete sides of the pen. It's hard to imagine that the trout enjoy being in the hatchery. But it is still exciting to watch the fish jump as I empty my hand of pellets and wipe the brown residue on my jeans.

A few feet from the pools, I see a sign describing the life cycle of the trout. Five pictures are displayed in a circle, with arrows connecting them. The female hen trout lays hundreds of eggs on the streambed that are fertilized by the male jack. The trout hatch and grow from tiny alevins that live off their yolk sac, to one-inch fry, to fingerlings. Next comes the parr stage, signified by "parr bars," which are vertical markings on the sides of the fish. By the age of two, the adult trout are ready to spawn and begin a new generation.

Glancing at the sign one last time, I am struck by the arrows connecting each stage of the trout's life, from birth to death and the birth of a new generation. The life of all creatures, piscine and human alike, is a circle, a never-ending journey. My mind drifts to the verse from the book of Ecclesiastes, written by King Solomon, and made famous in our time by the Byrds: "To every thing there is a season, and a time to every purpose under heaven. A time to be born and a time to die (3:1–2)."

A glance at my watch lifts me from my reverie and produces a sudden burst of anxiety. It's 3:30p.m., I'm a half mile from my car, my rod is not even put together, and the beats on the stream will be given out in an hour!

I quickly return to the car, where I see other anglers preparing for a day on the Connetquot. A half dozen men and women stand before open trunks and lowered tailgates, donning vests, putting together rods, and attaching leaders.

I feel a spike of adrenaline at the prospect of being on the stream so soon. But then I pause and take a breath. I need to take it slow, to be methodical in my preparation, and to ensure that I bring everything I need for a few hours on the stream. Because I've made mistakes before. A few months ago, I was so ready to get out of the house and to the river that I left my rod at home! I was pretty frustrated, but I went for a relaxing hike in the woods anyway. Then there was the time in Argentina when I was so excited to get out on the river that I put black reel grease on my favorite fly, completely destroying it. That's why we always tie more than one.

Hoping to avoid these pitfalls of the past, I slow down and begin to gear up. I put on a pair of thick green wool socks, washed so many times they are faded and stretched like a comfortable pair of jeans. Waders come up to the chest, followed by rubber-soled boots with tiny metal spikes. I switched to rubber soles a few years ago when I learned that the felt-soled boots spread invasive species of algae and crustaceans that can harm stream ecology and, therefore, the trout that live in those streams.

Next I clip my wading staff around my waist, don my vest, and attach my net to the magnetic clip on the back. I learned the value of the net clip one day after landing a large trout. I was holding the fish in one hand while removing the hook with my other so I could take a quick picture with my cell phone camera. I glanced up to see my expensive, polished wood-framed net floating downstream and out of reach.

No trip to the stream would be complete without my blue fishing hat with the large yellow *C.* I bought it at a Cabela's store on my way to Gettysburg, Pennsylvania, where I was to meet Ken Lokensgard, whom I like to call "the fly-fishing professor."

Ken was raised in Montana, a mecca of American fly-fishing. He grew up casting flies on the Big Blackfoot and Madison Rivers. Inspired by the Native Americans of his home state, he received his PhD in the religion and rituals of the Blackfeet peoples of Montana.

A few years ago, Ken invited me to come as a guest speaker for his undergraduate class at Gettysburg College on fly-fishing and religion, probably the only such class in existence in any institution of higher learning in the United States. On a Tuesday in May, ten undergraduates and I talked about religion and fly-fishing and debated the humane treatment of trout, including whether it is morally correct to stuff and mount a five-pound trout that you catch (I would rather release such a beautiful fish back to the stream).

The next day I had a chance to try out my new blue fishing hat when Ken and I fished the Letort Spring

Run, one of the famous limestone creeks of central Pennsylvania. We saw a black mailbox right next to the stream, and Ken showed me the tiny black pocketbook in it, filled with business cards of all sorts of people who had cast a line on these famous waters. As the Letort is known for an incredibly selective population of brown trout, we came up empty that day. Even a fly-fishing rabbi and professor are sometimes no match for the wily trout of the stream.

Today my blue Cabela's fly-fishing hat is worn, the color faded and the edges frayed from many trips to the stream and the occasional spin in the washing machine. But I would never wear anything else. As I dig the hat out of the green duffle, I remember that trip to the Letort Spring Run and how a professor from Montana and a rabbi from New York became friends fishing together in rural Pennsylvania.

With my hat on my head, standing before my open trunk at the state park, I finally pick up my fly rod, removing its four parts from the hard black canvas case. I examine the reel seat and my ugly (but hopefully effective) epoxy repair from this morning. The gray glue is dry and hard. I put together the rod and tighten the reel into the repaired seat. It holds firm. We're looking good so far, but who knows what will happen out on the water.

I pull the yellow fluorescent fly line through the guides of the fly rod and attach the clear leader and tippet. Reaching for my dry-fly box, I pull out the fly that I call "old reliable," a brown Elk Hair Caddis. With its straight, stiff elk hairs pressed down flat like the wings of the insect, the trout see an irresistible imitation of the caddis. A part of me also realizes that this brown fly looks a lot like the brown corn pellets that the trout feast on at the hatchery. Whatever the reason for its success, I have come to love this fly for all of the memories of fish that have risen to it.

I slip on polarized sunglasses that cut water glare and allow me to see into the stream, put on a coat of sunscreen, and complete the outfitting with a liberal spray of bug juice. I slip a bottle of water in my vest and put my cell phone in a small Ziploc bag in my waders pocket. Ten minutes ago I was just a normal guy in jeans and a T-shirt. Now I am a fly-fisherman, fully decked out, ready for the water.

At 4:25p.m. I walk up to the shack at the entrance to the park where the beats will be given out. Six anglers, including myself, stand before the tiny drive-though window, which is closed. A stern-looking woman behind the glass controls our fishing destiny, yet seems to do so without much regard for us. I suppose that dealing with anxious anglers for many years has added a few frown lines to her brow.

As the time creeps toward 4:30p.m., we stand only a few feet from each other in total silence. We are a half dozen grown men and women with jobs, spouses, children, and responsibilities. But today we are fully decked out in fishing gear, standing anxiously before a tiny window at a state park.

Perhaps it is my competitive nature, but the moment of selecting your beat seems to be one of supreme importance. I want to be in a good spot on the river, to see rising fish, to hold a few in my hands before releasing them. I am sure that not all of the beats will be good, and I want the best one. I want to win.

Finally, the tiny window opens, and the first name is called. A middle-aged man steps forward, greets the Giver of the Beats, and hands over a twenty dollar bill (regrettably you have to pay to fish this stream). He selects beat number 11, a fine choice. The park official turns around to face a large map of the river, on which over two dozen numbers indicate the beats. She moves a tiny red round magnet to cover number 11, indicating that that beat is taken. A woman is called next and chooses number 10, also a good spot.

This is all fine with me, because I am third in line and neither of the two previous anglers took my favorite spot. After hearing a gruff-sounding and slightly mispronounced "Eisenkramer," I step up to the window. I smile at the woman behind the desk, hand over the money, and say: "Seven, please." As a rabbi who celebrates the Sabbath on the seventh day, I'll soon be casting my flies on beat number 7 to trout that live for seven years. Everything seems to be coming together.

I take a quick glance at the piece of paper with beat number 7 written down and see that sunset is marked as beginning at 7:30p.m., the time when the day of fishing will end. That is three hours from now, and I still have a half-hour hike to the stream. I walk up the drive into the park. I once again pass the familiar landmarks, the large wooden house that was the sportsmen's club, the hard bench in front of the oval lake, and the small dam and old gristmill that a hundred years ago used the power of the river to grind wheat into flour.

In a few minutes, I am in the woods, and signs of civilization begin to recede. The dirt path stretches ahead due north. I am already starting to sweat. While waders, boots, and a vest are great for standing in 40-degree spring-fed trout water, they make lugging yourself and your fishing gear a mile through the woods cumbersome and hot.

The trees of Long Island are bare, giving the forest a sense of openness and potential. It is only April 3, and spring has not arrived. Yet glancing into the woods, I see a few stout green plants with wide leaves peeking through the soil. The early spring skunk cabbage reminds me of the hostas I planted in my patio garden.

A week ago, as spring began to creep into the Northeast, I drove to a local nursery to pick up a rosebush and two hostas. I could not remember the last time I planted something in the ground. My grandfather, may his memory be for a blessing, was a proficient gardener. In his large backyard in St. Louis, he grew dark red tomatoes along with carrots, blackberries, apples, and peaches. He even grew grapevines successfully. My grandfather loved singing the Sabbath Kiddush prayer over the wine each Friday evening, and I always thought this is why he chose to plant grapes in St. Louis, of all places.

As I stood before the dirt on our patio preparing to plant, I tried to think how my grandpa Henry would do it. Like my grandfather, like the Jews of the kibbutz in Israel, like my ancient ancestors in biblical times, I tilled the soil and dug a hole. A teaching of Rabbi Yohanan came to mind: "If you have a sapling in your hand and someone says to you that the Messiah has come, stay and complete the planting and then go greet the Messiah."

And then it was done. I had planted a tree (well, a rosebush and two hostas to be exact). I hope that all summer, my hostas will grow and my roses will bloom in the hot sun.

That same sun that makes the roses open has now made me sweat for thirty minutes as my feet take me through the forest and up the sandy path. A wooden gate stands before me, really just a long wooden bar between two stumps. This is the entrance to the river and the beats. I duck under the bar and enter the final dirt path. Another twenty feet, and the stream comes into view.

To my right, I see a wooden dock jutting ten or so feet into the water. It is three feet wide and made of wooden planks with gaps between, like the spaces between the bare trees in the forest that I just traversed. On the first plank, I see a yellow, spray-painted number 7. I walk up to the dock, sit down and have a good long drink of water.

Fifty miles from New York City by car, two restorative hours spent at the lake and the hatchery, a few tense moments in front of a state park shack, a half hour by foot, and a million light-years away from my ordinary life, I am finally at the river. It's time to go fishing.

## Reflection Questions

1.  The rivers where trout live are often far from the cities, towns, and other places where we spend most of our time. What journeys have you taken far from home? What trips have you taken that have enriched your life?

2.  On a fishing trip, we encounter familiar landmarks like a clubhouse in front of a lake or a tall mountain along the road. What are some of your favorite landmarks? How do they frame and add meaning to your travels?

3.  At the fly-fishing store, anglers can seek advice, find camaraderie, and see old friends. Who do you turn to for advice in your life? What journeys

have been shared with friends, and how has that enriched the experience?

# Exercise: Meditative Walking to the River[1]

1. While standing still in wilderness, focus on your breath. You might listen for the subtle sound of breathing, notice the rising and falling of the belly and chest, or focus on the sensation of air passing through the nostrils. When thoughts arise, gently let them go and return to the breath.

2. After a minute, leave half your attention on the breath and place the other half on the bottoms of your feet. Feel the pressure of your body on the earth; notice the constant adjustments your muscles make to maintain balance.

3. After another minute, shift your focus once again. Place 25 percent of your awareness on your breath, another 25 percent on the soles of your feet, and 50 percent on the world around you. Begin to walk, taking in all the sounds and sights of the land you are traversing.

4. When your mind wanders and focus fades, try not to get angry at yourself. This happens to everyone, no matter how experienced at meditative walking. Gently return your attention to the breath and the soles of your feet, then look, listen, and continue on.

# CHAPTER THREE

# BEING THERE

## WADING INTO THE STREAM AND INTO YOURSELF

*To go fishing is the chance to wash one's soul with pure air, with the rush of the brook, or with the shimmer of sun on blue water. It brings meekness and inspiration from the decency of nature, charity toward tackle-makers, patience toward fish, a mockery of profits and egos, a quieting of hate, a rejoicing that you do not have to decide a darned thing until next week. And it is discipline in the equality of men—for all men are equal before fish.*

*—Herbert Hoover (1874–1964), thirty-first president of the United States*

# RABBI ERIC: STREAM AND SPIRIT

The Connetquot River flows north to south from a hidden spring somewhere in suburban Long Island, through a state park, the hatchery, and the two dozen or so wooden docks that mark the beats, into the large lake in front of the wooden clubhouse, and then out to the Atlantic Ocean. At dock number 7, the stream is perhaps 20 feet wide, with trees pushing right to the edge of the water. My beat encompasses a small section of the river, about 50 feet in each direction from the dock. My trout paradise is 20 feet wide and a 100 feet long. At 200 square feet, it is the same size as a small studio apartment in Manhattan—but the twenty dollar rental fee for the stream is much cheaper than New York City apartment prices!

The studio-sized stream around dock number 7 is probably home to at least two dozen 'bows and browns, with the occasional brookie as well. The water runs cold and deep, with a slight current and the occasional riffle.

As I stand before the river, I begin to strategize. You can have the most beautifully tied fly and elegant cast, but if your approach to the stream is loud and you spook the fish, all your efforts will be for naught. Trout swim against the current and, with eyes on the sides of their heads, use their vision as a primary way to detect danger. The path of their vision points upward, taking the shape of an inverted cone, with the point located at the surface of their eye, so that their field of vision widens the farther away it gets. This is a good natural strategy for a creature that lives underwater and takes much of its food from the water's surface above it. Knowing this, I try to stand as far from the fish as possible to avoid detection.

The sun is still relatively high in the sky. With my polarized glasses blocking out the glare, I see the streambed clearly, its sandy bottom strewn with rocks and the occasional outgrowth of dark-green wavy algae. As I expected, there are no trout in the sun-drenched parts of the river. But the trees on the opposite shore from the dock are blocking the sun and have created a long thin stretch of shade. My polarized glasses cannot pierce those shadows, but I know that's where the trout are.

Then I hear a light plop. My eyes dart up and down the shady strip of water. I see a tiny round circle, expanding slowly from its center. A trout has risen. I glance down at "old reliable," the brown Elk Hair Caddis fly that I tied on the line back at the car. I do not see many bugs on the stream; it is still too hot for a surface hatch. But since the trout did rise, I'll give my caddis a try anyway.

The fish is on the opposite shore, about twenty feet downstream from the dock where I am sitting. All I need to do is wade into the stream a few feet and cast straight across the river. Always cognizant of how easy it is to "spook" a fish, I pause for a moment before entering the water. I try to channel a mystical ancient vision of a fish hunter, at one with the river, moving with grace and in silence. Or at the very least I try to be a little more subtle than your basic Elmer Fudd type.

I take one careful step into the river. At first contact with the water, the remaining sweat on my brow is lost to the bite of the cold, spring-fed stream. The cold is jarring. I appreciate anew my neoprene chest waders and thick green wool socks that will keep me warm until sunset. I take a few more steps and the water rises higher, now to my waist. The bite of the cold fades, and I feel a sense of peace begin to spread through my limbs. The pure water washes away all of my worries and replaces them with an abiding sense of well-being. It is as if all of my troubles are flowing downstream now, receding into the distance.

Standing waist deep in the cold river, I am reminded of a time when I dunked in the *mikvah,* the Jewish ritual bath. I was living in Jerusalem, in my first year of rabbinical studies. I had just learned about the centuries-old Jewish mystical custom of immersing oneself in cold water right before the Sabbath as a way to greet the holy day. I walked the few blocks from our rental apartment in Rechavia, a beautiful neighborhood of trees and short buildings, past the home of the president of Israel, with its tall gates and security guards, and to a small anonymous building. Only in Jerusalem are you within walking distance of a ritual bath.

I stood alone in a small room before a tiny pool, the mikvah. As is customary, I removed all clothing and jewelry and immersed myself completely in the water, so that it covered every inch of my body. I offered the blessing, thanking God for the privilege of immersing myself in the holy waters. I paused for a moment, in silence, absorbing the chill and preparing to let go of the week and welcome in the Sabbath with joy.

Standing in the trout stream, I remember that the cold waters of the mikvah are called *mayim chaim,* waters of life. Jewish law states that the waters must connect to a natural source, such as collected rainwater. The trout stream is likewise *mayim chaim,* a life-giving place, one that sustains insects and fish, but also replenishes and nourishes the soul of the angler.

A second small plop lifts me from my reverie, and I see what is probably the same fish rising in the shade across the stream. I take out "old reliable" from the tiny metal ring holder at the base of my fly rod and drop him in the stream. He floats comfortably, aided by the gooey "fly-float" oil that I applied a few moments ago.

I pull out a long length of fluorescent-green fly line from the reel, at least twenty-five feet. Holding the soft cork rod butt in my right hand and the loosened line coiled in my left, I lift up the rod tip until it is slightly behind my head at the two o'clock position for the backcast. As my hand travels past my eyes, I catch a glimpse of the gray blob of glue holding the reel in place. This is the moment of truth. Will my fly-rod repair from this morning work?

The green fly line lifts from the water and sails past my right ear. The clear leader straightens and the caddis fly on the end stretches as far back behind me as the line will allow. I feel the tension of the fully extended line in my arm and shoulder. I smoothly move my arm forward, to the ten o'clock position slightly in front of my head. The fluorescent-green fly line forms a long, narrow loop, then wraps over itself in midair, as the loop moves farther from the rod and toward my shady target. Finally, the clear leader drops down softly on the stream's surface, unrolling to the end. A metal hook, wrapped in brown elk hair, lands delicately on the water. The fly is floating. I exhale. I feel the tension drain in my lungs, like the tension that was released in the fly line that I just cast, like the tension from my normal life that I feel continuing to melt away.

Then I smile, because the rod repair held. Each time I cast my St. Croix rod from now on, I will see the small gray blob of glue, and I will remember the time when my fly rod broke the morning that I decided to go fishing and I was able to fix it with my own hands.

The caddis fly landed in the shady area about fifteen feet upstream from the spot of the last rise. I was hoping to get it a little closer, within five feet, so that the trout would strike quickly again. I watch the fly drift down slowly with the current. It floats past the "kill zone," and nothing happens. A moment later, the fly is well downstream, no longer drifting naturally but held in place by the fly line, and it is time to cast once more.

As the fly shoots past my head again, I begin to "false cast," moving the line forward and back in the air without letting the fly touch the water. False casting allows the angler to shoot out more line and change the direction of the cast; it also dries out the fly. It also just feels good to keep casting, to watch the line sail back and forth in graceful loops in the air, and to feel the tension and movement.

As I continue to false cast, I hear the Elk Hair Caddis zip back and forth, and I feel for a moment transported to another river, one that I only know from the movie screen. In my mind, I see wide banks and the fast currents of the Big Blackfoot of Montana from *A River Runs Through It.* Known affectionately as "The Movie" to many anglers, the film tells the tale of a fly-fishing minister, Revered Maclean, and his two sons, Paul and Norman, in early twentieth-century Montana.

In my mind's eye, I see a tanned forearm moving the rod forward, the line gracefully entering its loop, the fly headed out into river. I hear the film score, the soft piano music accompanying this perfect moment of motion. The fly lands softly in a small flat pool surrounded by riffles. In an instant, it is swallowed by a large mouth coming to the surface.

As my fly line continues its path back and forth in the air, I also see myself once again sitting in the

Hi-Pointe Theatre in St. Louis, watching *A River Runs Through It,* captivated and absorbed by this new type of fishing that I had never experienced before. Growing up, I fished the bass lakes with my dad. When "The Movie" came out I was eighteen years old and on my way to college in Boston. The idea of becoming a rabbi was just beginning to form in my mind. In the dark movie theater, I also discovered a second passion, fly-fishing, which would consume my few precious free hours of the spring and summer months. That day I also found a kindred spirit in the Reverend Maclean, a fellow fly-fishing clergyman.

Memories of St. Louis and Montana fade, and I am back on the Connetquot, telling myself: "One more false cast, and I'll let the fly go." The caddis sails behind me in perfect rhythm. As I move my arm to shoot the fly forward, the line comes to a harsh and abrupt stop. My shoulders drop, I turn around, and I see that my fly is caught in a tree. You would think that after a dozen times fishing beat number 7 on the Connetquot River, I would remember to use my roll cast to account for tight stream conditions. But caught up in the moment, wanting to relive the casting of my fly-fishing heroes, the Macleans of Montana, I chose the traditional forward cast, and I hooked a branch.

I try to pull the fly free to no avail. Any harder and I will break the line. So I carefully step out of the water, trying not to spook the fish, and walk over to the offending tree. My caddis fly is caught around a small branch, my leader wound in the leaves, and even the fly line is tangled in the tree. What a mess.

I take a deep breath to calm down and begin the laborious process of untangling the fly. In my impatience and desire to quickly return to the stream and the rising trout, I want to just yank the line. But that maneuver usually ends with a lost fly and a knotted and unusable leader. I have learned that it is best to move slowly, to wind the fly in and out of its loops and curves until it is straight once again.

So I work carefully and methodically to untangle the line. It is the same way I've learned to deal with other problems in life that require this type of patience. As a rabbi, I am always trying to help people untangle complex situations in their lives: spiritual crises, difficult relationships with their loved ones, and other everyday challenges. I, too, have made mistakes that have created difficult knots: speaking harsh words in times of stress and anxiety, harming those I love with word and deed, and being too slow to forgive when hurt myself. As I work to untangle my fly, I remind myself that pulling too hard never works. But if I just try to fix my problems one step and one tangled loop at a time, there is the possibility of straightening them out and beginning anew.

As I step back into the stream, I hear a third plop and glance into the shade. I assume it is the same trout rising once again, this time surely out of spite and chutzpah. I raise the rod slowly, ensuring that the line will remain on the water and will not sail behind me. With a snappy forward movement of my arm, I send the line in a large loop, a roll cast unfolding onto the river. The fly lands only a few feet upstream of the rise of a moment ago. I hear a slap on the water, my caddis fly disappears, and the line goes taut. I have hooked my first fish of the day.

A firm but not too hard upward pull of the rod sets the hook, and I begin to reel in the fish. Most often I can tell right away how big the fish is on my line. A six- or eight-inch trout cannot put up much resistance and is quickly brought to the net. In the twelve- to sixteen-inch range, the trout will run, and I have to be careful not to snap the line. Trying to reel in a truly large trout is like trying to pull a tank through the water. You cannot really move a fish this size; you just have to keep him out of trouble spots in the stream and wait until he wears himself out.

The fish on the end of my line today is no monster; it feels about medium-sized. I let it run a bit and begin to reel it in. When the trout is only a few feet away, I pull the net from its magnetic holder, lower it into the water, and pull up a nice-sized brown trout.

While the fish is out of its element, I take additional precautions to ensure that it will survive. I had already pushed down the barb on the hook to make it easier to remove from the mouth of the trout. I did not overplay the fish. Now, with the brownie in the net,

I dunk my hands in the water before handling it so as not to damage its skin with the oils from my hand. I remove the hook with the fishing forceps (which look exactly like surgeon's forceps, a doctor friend told me), and I take a quick picture with my cell phone camera.

Then I pause and take a moment to really look at the fish. Trout are amazing creatures, lean and muscular with graceful fins and beautiful coloring. This brownie has a yellowish tinge with a few red and orange spots sprinkled among many large black dots. I smile once again as I look at this perfect fish in my hands, a miracle of creation, a gift from our natural world. I offer a quiet blessing, thanking God for the river, the fish, and the privilege to stand in a stream and hold a trout.

As I lean down to return the fish to the water, I wonder for a moment if this trout is a male or female, and my smile begins to fade a bit. Not two years ago, on beat number 7 of the Connetquot, I caught another brown trout, about the same size, and I decided to keep it. The stream regulations allow anglers to take home two fish a day, and this was my first catch.

On the rare occasion when I decide to take home a fish, I try to be as humane as possible. I never used a creel, thinking it cruel to keep a fish alive for hours, attached to a metal chain. To kill the fish, some anglers use a small wooden mallet called a "priest," named for the fact that you are giving the fish its last rites. I use a very sharp knife, influenced by the Jewish dietary laws, known as *kashrut.* For beef to be kosher, the butcher must show respect to the animal and end its life quickly, with the least amount of pain possible. The Jewish butcher uses an extremely sharp knife with no nicks or imperfections. This is the mitzvah of *tzaar ba'alei chaim,* which means preventing unnecessary pain to animals.

After the great flood, God told Noah that humans may consume animals as long as they sacrifice a part of the animal to God in thanksgiving. I eat beef, chicken, and fish, and I believe that consuming animals is a necessary part of being human. I love the taste of rainbow trout fillets, brushed with olive oil and sprinkled with salt and broiled to perfection. But it is never fun to do the killing myself, and I have always felt guilty.

That day two years ago on the Connetquot, I carried the brown trout in my net into the forest to clean it, finding a spot well off of the stream so as not to pollute the river. I killed it quickly and as humanely as possible. When I opened the trout's belly with my knife, I discovered hundreds of small orange eggs. The fish was pregnant.

I thought of the teaching of the rabbis: He who kills a person, it is as if he has destroyed an entire world. I had killed one fish. But I also destroyed hundreds of eggs and the possibility of just as many trout filling the river. I placed the fillets in a cooler filled with ice that I had lugged the entire mile from my car back at the entrance to the state park. I threw the carcass into the forest, to be eaten and recycled by nature. Then I stopped and caught my breath; it was always stressful and hard to kill a trout.

Standing once again on beat number 7 on the Connetquot, I take a final look at the beautiful brown trout. At this moment I hold the power of life and death in my hands. I bend down toward the stream, stretch out my arm, release my grip, and watch as the brown trout swims back into the depths.

There are many good reasons to practice catch-and-release fishing. If we kept every fish that we caught, the streams would soon be empty of trout. Catch-and-release also helps preserve the streams. I have seen rivers littered with fish carcasses, their pristine ecosystems damaged by thoughtless anglers. But for me, returning a trout to the stream is an act that makes me feel humane rather than simply human and helps me move closer to the compassion that emanates from my divine maker.

By now the sun has sunk low in the sky, yet I am still casting on beat number 7. In the last few hours, I caught a couple more fish and released them. Most days I do not keep count because fly-fishing means more to me than the number of fish brought to the net. Today, I fished every riffle and pool on my beat. I switched from a brown Elk Hair Caddis fly to a black and white Griffith's Gnat dry fly until the fish stopped rising. Then, I tied on a red Copper John underwater nymph and a beadhead Prince Nymph, both with floating strike indicators, which brought two rainbows to the net.

I have cast for hours, with only short breaks for water to stay hydrated and for snacks to keep up my energy level. The cold water and the smooth action of the fly rod are hypnotic. I am in an altered state, the fly-casting a form of meditation, easing my troubles and focusing my mind.

As my day of fly-fishing nears its end, I softly sing the words of the Shema, the central prayer in Judaism: *Shema Yisrael Adonai Eloheinu, Adonai Echad*—Hear O Israel, Adonai is our God, Adonai is One. God is one. I, too, am one, alone on the stream, singular, soaking in the solitude.

I false cast again and again, the fly floating in the air back and forth in perfect rhythm. In my mind I hear the words of Norman Maclean, the son of a fly-fishing minister from Montana: "In the Arctic half-light of the canyon, all existence fades to a being with my soul and memories and the sounds of the Big Blackfoot River and a four-count rhythm and the hope that a fish will rise. Eventually, all things merge into one, and a river runs through it."

Standing in a river that runs through Long Island, I, too, am a part of this grand oneness.

# REVEREND MIKE: FISHING INTO THE MYSTERY

Moving blood has a sound as it courses through our bodies. As a cardiologist, I have spent a lifetime listening to that sound, learning its mysteries and its wonder as it tells me a story. I can tell in a moment if a valve is leaking, if an artery is kinked or obstructed, or if flow is smooth and unobstructed.

The simulators that are used in medical education now do not, in my mind, capture the nuances and mystery of these ever-so-gorgeous sounds. Simulators sound, well, artificial. There is no other way to put it. They are not living, breathing, hurting, curious, cautious. They are not alive. There is nothing more satisfying than listening to the music of the human body and being able to piece together a story of wonder, of brokenness, and of the possibilities of wholeness.

I suppose this may be one of the many ways that the "art" of medicine draws so many of us in to start with. How are these lovely sounds made? What stories can they tell us of this life in our hands? How can we listen to this gift we are now given, and learn the stories they tell us time and time again? Blood is, of course, nothing but water with a few extra things thrown in for good measure. Like water, it is the life force of the universe. And so, it is the sound of water that we all come home to when we walk into a river.

My house in Colorado sits in a secluded valley. In the mornings I experience profound silence time and time again. Before the wind starts, the aspens are still. The road noise is muffled by the valley contours. The birds are not fully awake yet. The deer and elk that may be sneaking along my property step so softly that not a leaf or twig makes a noise.

It is pure, soft, silence that surrounds me as I begin to prepare for a trip to the river. It is the silence of comfort, of peace, of prayer. It is wordless, imageless, dreamless. It is the place of longing, of desire, of ultimate growth. I have often felt that we are inundated with noise pollution—not necessarily of machinery and of civilization but of inane conversation, useless arguments, meaningless words. We need to find the time and space and place to be still and silent.

Yet, when I arrive at the water, silence is replaced by nothing less than a sound that is oh-so-similar to the sound of blood coursing through our arteries and veins. It is the sound of water coursing through our planet. It is the sound of our planet's life force. I open the door of my car and walk to the water. And the sounds of the river begin to whisper their stories to me. I close my eyes and listen.

In a moment I can tell how high the flow is, and whether there are new fallen trees changing the shape of the river. I can begin to imagine the soft water flowing around, over, and under the rocks that, in a sense, are alive. I can almost hear the fish moving around quietly, waiting for the breakfast bell to ring. Occasionally I will hear the sip, the splash, or something ever so soft that tells me that water is the source of life. If I am still enough, I often hear the sound of my own breath and my own heartbeat. Yes, I am alive. This is the place where I feel it the most and know it with every cell in my body.

Just last night I had only been in the water a few minutes, but heard something different, something soft, that sounded "out of place" among the normal sounds of the river. I looked above the far bank and saw two large mule deer does and their fawns sneaking down the ledge and carefully stepping into the water. The first doe's eyes met mine. She looked at me, and decided that although she knew I was in her place, I was no threat to her. So she led her family into the water and crossed the river not thirty feet from where I was fishing. The fawns looked curiously at me with wide-eyed wonder and no hint of fear.

The sound of them floundering along the rocky bottom of the stream was so different from the sound of the steps of their mothers, who seemed to know intuitively where to place their feet. Like novice anglers, the fawns floundered around, making lots of silly but somehow sweet noise in the water.

We all were there, immersed in water, the sound of silence and the sound of life. It is so much like the sound of our blood, and time after time it tells us a story we need to hear. Life always wins out, and water and blood may be one of the ways that we finally see how that story is told in our own lives.

This morning I sit on the river bank, eyes closed, listening to both water and blood, and offer a simple prayer of surrender that is analogous to Morning Prayer in the Episcopal Book of Common Prayer:

> *Let the earth glorify the Lord,*
> *praise him and highly exalt him for ever.*
> *Glorify the Lord, O mountains and hills,*
> *and all that grows upon the earth,*
> *praise him and highly exalt him for ever.*
> *Glorify the Lord, O springs of water, seas, and*
> *streams,*
> *O whales and all that move in the waters.*

A good day on the river is often a result of how centered I am, how willing I am to surrender my ego and will. When I am able to do that, the magic simply happens. Intuition supplants the analytical.

If I don't take the time to offer this prayer of "surrender," then my time on the water is not as healing. Emotionally, I wind up in a place that is not all that different from the place I left behind. I need a period of stillness, of silence, of "pre" preparation before I actually immerse myself in the river. Thomas Merton, a Catholic monk and mystic, realized that we cannot encounter the world in any meaningful healing way until we find the time to live in stillness. In *Dialogues with Silence,* he says, "Let me rest in Your will and be silent. Then the light of Your joy will warm my life. Its fire will burn in my heart. This is what I live for. Amen, amen."[1]

After prayer, I indulge in another ritual. I stand on the bank and observe my surroundings for fifteen or twenty minutes. I feel the wind, look for browsing, rising fish, and get a feel for the flow rates. I look under rocks for the life-forms that fish seek. I want to feel the life of the fish in my body, to sense their iron wills and wily natures, to give thanks for the day I have been given.

Fifteen minutes later I don't see any flying bugs, but that's okay. I know they'll come. I'll just have to wile away the time until then. I grab my nymph rig and walk gently into the water. When the hatch emerges, I will switch to the appropriate dry fly.

My fly vest is filled with boxes of flies arranged by the season and bugs: nymphs in one box and dries in another, arranged loosely by size and color. I always have plenty of 6X–7X tippet, snippets, goop, dessicant for flotation and added visibility, and extra leaders in case I get a major equipment malfunction.

I usually carry a small waterproof camera—not to take fish pictures so much as to capture the glory of the small, unexpected moments. I was fishing alone one winter day, surrounded by snow and silence, when I looked about thirty yards to my right and saw a magnificent royal 6x6 bull elk sipping at the water's edge. He looked at me quietly and intensely. I bowed my head to him. He kept drinking and gently walked back into the forest from where he had come. It is moments like that that transcend the actual fishing that we are given from time to time. Those are the moments of incarnate glory that every angler gets to witness if he or she is fortunate enough. They seem to come at the times when we need them the very most.

I arrive at my favorite pool on the Frying Pan, affectionately named the Eagles Nest Pool after a pair of bald eagles that nested for years on lovely red rock outcropping on the far side of the pool. Even though they have been gone for years, I can still see them in my mind's eye watching us frail humans invade their territory.

It is an unusual run, for the lower section below the pull-out is easily seen and easily waded and has some nice fishing. But the upper section is hidden by a large conifer tree and a deep willow break, so access is a bit trickier and easy to miss if you don't know where to look for the trail down to the water. But when I walk that trail and emerge into the loveliest pool in the world, I begin to be transformed.

The ideal flow rates for this part of the river would be about 200 cfs. It is a wide pool with nice shelves on both sides and a good deep run down the middle. Higher water makes crossing hard but not undoable.

The water will be anywhere from my mid-calf to slightly above my knees—ideal to feel the cold water holding me firmly in place as I plant my feet on the rocks below.

And then the casting begins—almost always with one or two dry flies to start with. Even if I do not see any rising or working fish or flies in the air, I almost always start with a dry-fly rig. It seems to help me center quicker and find my pace and rhythm, as opposed to a nymph rig with a strike indicator. Starting with a nymph rig just doesn't seem quite "right" to me. But I am not above switching after thirty minutes or so!

And the casts begin. For me, the life is in the back cast and proper load of the rod. That is where I am convinced most novices make the most mistakes. Taking time on the back cast and letting the rod completely load and the line lie straight back is such a sweet, pure, physical moment of perfection. It makes the rest of the cast go so much better, yet we often want to rush it.

It is much like my golf swing in that regard. Rushing forward is no good at all. Let it be. Let it happen. Breathe. Take your time. Experience the perfection of physics in your hands. The fish will be there when the fly arrives; there is no rush at all. And finally, when the forward part of the cast begins, what draws me into the moment is the sound.

I can tell by the sound if my line is being shot forward with life and grace. It slices through the air, making a pure, sweet, swishing sound. There is nothing quite like it. Letting the line go with my left hand, feeling it lie out like a razor, and watching the dry fly land softly brings me to the heart of myself. If I have read the water right and made just the right number of false casts to get enough line out, I am amazed at how often a trout rises to the first cast. Not every time, of course, for such perfection is not to be found in this lifetime. It is enough to savor the moment, to rest in its grace, to dwell in its freedom.

We are all born of water, and thus, are water creatures from our very moment of conception. The human body, just like our planet, is more than 75 percent water. Our cells and bodies arise from that mysterious liquid. I've often thought that instead of the phrase "dust to dust" a more appropriate and lovely phrase would be "water to water": we are born, we live, and we die in water. They may put our bodies in dust eventually, but for anglers, our true home is in the waters that sustain our lives and our planet, in what the Episcopal Book of Common Prayer calls "this fragile earth, our island home."

## Reflection Questions

1. The rhythmic casting of the fly rod can be a meditative practice. What activities in your life

aid in finding your center? How do these help relieve stress and ease tension?

2. When fly-fishing alone on the stream, we encounter silence and solitude, rare gifts in our ever-noisy world. How does the quiet of the stream benefit us? What are some ways that we can bring more solitude into our lives?

3. Holding a trout in your hand is a moment when you experience the immediacy of life and death, as the trout's life hangs in the balance. When have you encountered the reality of life and death, when human mortality appeared right before you? What lessons did you learn from that experience?

4. What do your senses tell you when you "arrive" at your home? What memories do those senses bring out from your past as well as present?

5. Which of your senses is the most highly tuned to the environment where you experience grace?

# Exercise: The Basics of Fly-Casting

1. Let out twenty-five feet of line in front of you. Practice out of the water and without a fly on the line so that you won't have to worry about getting caught up in anything.

2. Grip your rod as if you were shaking hands with it. Set the rod's handle in your palm and close

your fingers around it, keeping your thumb on top.

3. Face the direction that you want to cast, putting your weight on the balls of your feet. Keep your wrist still and stiff; don't allow it to bend. Your elbow, not your shoulder, should be your pivot point. Picture hammering a nail.

4. Think of the movement of your arm in casting as being like that of a clock's hands. If you view an angler from his or her left profile, the caster will move the rod between eleven o'clock on the forward cast and one o'clock on the back cast.

5. Hold the rod at eleven o'clock to begin. From the tip, the loose fly line should trace down the rod until you can grab it with your free hand. Hold and keep it above waist-level.

6. Pull the rod back to one o'clock, release the line and wait there until the line straightens behind you. Now accelerate the rod forward to eleven o'clock and wait for the loop formed by the arcing line to straighten out.

7. Bring the fingers of your free hand toward the reel and grasp the line between your index finger and thumb.

8. Pull in your outstretched line in 6-inch lengths so it forms a big excess loop right above the reel. You're not pulling more line off the reel or putting any back, you're simply gathering slack to ease

the next cast. Pull in only as much as you need to place your cast.

9. To end casting, stop with the forward cast at eleven o'clock. All the slack you pulled in will sail out with your fly (when you have one on the line), which should land right on your target. Assuming, of course, that you've been practicing.[2]

# Exercise: Improving your Fly-Casting with Lefty Kreh's Five Principles

*Note: The principles below were written by Bernard "Lefty" Kreh, well-known angler, photographer, and fly-fishing instructor.*

**Principle Number One:** The rod is a flexible lever which moves through varying arc lengths depending upon the casting distance required.

**Principle Number Two:** You cannot make a cast until you get the end of the line moving; and on the back cast, the end of the line should be lifted from the surface of the water before the cast is made.

**Principle Number Three:** The line and the fly are going to go in the direction in which you accelerate and stop the rod tip at the end of the cast.

**Principle Number Four:** The size of the fly line loop is determined only by the distance that you accelerate the rod tip at the end of the cast. And the faster that you accelerate over that distance, combined with a quick stop, the farther the cast will travel.

**Principle Number Five:** For long or more difficult casts, you will need to bring the rod well behind your body on the back cast. In order to do this, you should rotate your casting thumb away from its normal position on top of the rod about 45 degrees away from your body before initiating the back cast, and then take your forearm (never the wrist) straight back 180 degrees from the target.[3]

CHAPTER FOUR

# HOMECOMING

## PEACE AND HARMONY AT THE END OF THE DAY

*There is certainly something in fishing that tends to produce a gentleness of spirit, a pure serenity of mind.*

*—Washington Irving (1783–1859), American author*

# REVEREND MIKE: FISHING INTO THE MYSTERY

The day's end brings healing to a tired old body. If I have fished all day my back is tired, my eyes are gritty and burning, and my face is weathered. The fatigue is palpable, but so is the joy of being with friends or in silence on waters that heal. My hair is sticking out of my faded orange hat at crazy angles. More than likely I have a few tiny fly puncture sites on a finger here and there. I might well be dehydrated. I could be wet and cold or hot and sweaty. But in spite of the physical groans, my spirits and heart are soaring. It just doesn't get any better than this. Whether there were scores of fish caught or a skunking is totally irrelevant. If I got my act together and found my still spot, I have that "peace that passes all understanding" that is so hard to describe. It is a totality of being, a sensation of body, mind, and spirit in harmony.

One common sensation I am aware of is the changing nature of light on the water as the setting sun goes down. The shadows move across the water, the colors become more muted, and the air takes on a palpable texture. Light is so much a part of creation that we rarely pay attention to the way it shifts, changes, emerges, and softly fades. We take it for granted, like we do so many of the blessings we are given daily. Fishing seems to heighten my senses and make me more acutely aware of the ever-changing nature of light. We shall never get this day again, I say to myself. It has been a blessing and a gift, and now, it is gone. So be it. Be at peace.

As I move out of the water to the car, the rituals begin. If I have fished with friends, it is more or less the same, since we all have similar tastes. We sit around the rocks on the bank or in chairs we have brought and open a cold beer or pass a flask of Maker's Mark around. We may snack on a piece of cold cheese or an apple. More than likely we light up one last cigar that will last at least the thirty minutes it takes to let our bodies begin to recover and to replay the day. We describe in totally useless and fun detail the fish missed and caught. We talk about the wind, the rain, the sun, and the hatches. We are the ESPN *SportsCenter* team going over, in quite accurate and interesting detail, what the day was about. Invariably, the biggest fish is the one that got away—perhaps that particular riff is a part of every angler's gene pool. We may talk about the evening dinner plans, or how good the hot shower is going to feel. We may drift off into other things finally, but by unspoken agreement the one thing we do not discuss on the river is work. It may come up later over drinks, at home over supper, or in the morning over coffee. But river time is sacred space, and we all feel that we taint it by discussing work, answering e-mail, or worrying about things that are out of our control.

If I am alone, the rituals are similar but wordless. I may replay some of the fish in my mind. Being totally human and frail I will almost certainly visualize the missed fish or the stubborn refusal of my perfectly presented flies. I will likely enjoy a sip of good bourbon and a nice cigar on my own. Then I will remain still, in a place of wordless gratitude, enjoying the sound of the river and the peace of the place. I will often stretch out and place my hat under my head on a rock for some semblance of comfort. Then I simply breathe, listen, and watch. I may do a few minutes of centering prayer, the ancient Christian form of meditation. Often I will find myself saying the words from a Compline service—an ancient bedtime prayer form—from the New Zealand Prayer Book:

*My brothers and sisters,*
*our help is in the name of the eternal God,*
*who is making the heavens and the earth.*

*Dear God,*
*thank you for all that is good,*
*for our creation and our humanity,*
*for the stewardship you have given us of this*
 *planet earth,*
*for the gifts of life and of one another,*
*for your love which is unbounded and eternal.*
*O thou, most holy and beloved,*
*my Companion, my guide upon the way*
*my bright evening star.*
*We repent the wrongs we have done:*
*We have wounded your love.*
*O God, heal us.*
*We stumble in the darkness.*
*Light of the world transfigure us.*
*We forget that we are your home.*
*Spirit of God, dwell in us.*
*Eternal Spirit, living God,*
*in whom we live and move and have our being,*
*all that we are, have been, and shall be is known*
 *to you,*
*to the very secret of our hearts*
*and all that rises to trouble us.*
*Living flame, burn into us,*
*cleansing wind, blow through us,*
*fountain of water, well up within us,*
*that we may love and praise in deed and in truth.*

And so the day comes full circle. We end in our beginning—which is water. Our bodies and our spirits are full, and joy abides in the moments of wonder we had. The river will continue as it does, day after day, season after season. In a few million years it may be a totally different river, but for my brief span of life on this planet it has filled me up. Once again.

# RABBI ERIC: STREAM AND SPIRIT

The sun is sinking low in the sky, and my day of fly-fishing is nearing its end. Usually I head home before sunset. But on occasion I will fish past dark with the aid of a bright LED hiking light on an elastic band around my forehead.

Although I have heard that trout feast at night, I have never had much luck after dark. One moonless night while waist deep in the stream, I heard flapping sounds and looked up to see bats zooming past my head. Then I knew it was time to go home. Another time in the stream after dark I glanced up to see a large orange orb on the horizon; the moon was rising. For the next hour I cast blindly, hoping to hear the sound of a rising fish. Meanwhile, the moon made its way up the sky, and the stars came out. The earth and the river were calm and at peace.

Today I will not be fishing past dark, but I am beginning to think about the last cast. It is always a little sad for me to end a day of fishing, to stop doing something that I love. So I play a little game with myself, deciding that I'll take three more casts and reel in. Then I add another three casts. Some large multiple of three later, I finally call it a day.

Somewhere between last casts nine and twelve, the Connetquot River comes to life. With the sun below the tree line, the entire stream is covered in shade, and a half dozen fish are rising up and down the river. I briefly turn on the LED hiking light and shine it toward the stream to reveal dozens of tiny brown insects with large flat wings. I am standing in the middle of an evening caddis hatch, and the trout are feasting greedily. Now is the perfect time to use my brown Elk Hair Caddis and match the hatch. It looks like I'll have to delay that last cast a bit more.

Ten minutes and a few dozen casts later, I have not caught a thing. That's fly-fishing for you. You do everything right, you match the hatch, you do not spook the fish, you cast softly and gracefully, and you still get skunked. Maybe that is what keeps me coming back for more. Fly-fishing is a continuous challenge, one that engages my body and mind and helps ease the troubles of my soul.

On a previous trip to the Connetquot, I hooked a rainbow trout on my last cast. That was the way to end a day of fishing. Today I tell myself that if I can just hook one more trout, I'll head home. But it is not to be.

As I finally reel in for the day, I find myself thinking about endings. I know that as a mortal being, I will be unable to finish all that I would desire in fishing and in life. I may not be able to purchase that cabin on a Catskill river, or fish all of the great streams of

Montana and the American West, or visit the distant destinations that I read about where the trout grow huge, like New Zealand.

I think about what it will be like to make the last cast of my life. Moses lived to be 120, his eyes undimmed, his vigor unabated. God willing, I will live into such vibrant old age, fishing for many more decades. Then one day, I will take a final trip to my home waters. I will have a good day on the stream, maybe not catching as many trout as I would today in my thirties, but the decades of fishing experience will make up for the loss of youth and strength. After the last cast of that day, I will stop to say a blessing for the gift of life itself and for having experienced the fullness of the world.

Standing on dock number 7, rod in hand, ready to head home, I take one more moment to look at the river. I thank the trout, the stream, and the forest for another beautiful day of fishing. Then I start walking back to my car.

Now the fatigue sets in. It's still pretty hot, especially decked out in full waders. No longer buoyed by the water, I feel the full weight of my fishing gear. As my body heats up from the exercise, the smells of the day rise to my nostrils. My skin is covered in layers of dried sweat, suntan lotion, and bug repellant. Below all of these, I smell the stream, that same rich green natural scent that rose many hours ago this morning when I first opened my duffle bag and took out my vest.

Today, I have added another layer of river scent to my fly-fishing vest, like an age ring on a tree. I lift my hands to my face, and detect another familiar odor, one that I had hoped I would be able to breathe in this day: the pungent fishy smell of the trout that I held in my hands.

The walk back to the car is always slower than the walk to the stream. I am exhausted, and since my day of fishing is over, there is no need to rush. I walk the path away from dock number 7 and into the woods. I duck under the wooden gate and begin the long hike back on the sandy trail to the parking lot.

Then I hear a rustling in the woods. I look up to see four deer in the trees, about a hundred feet away. I stop. They are frozen, staring at me. I see the buck with his large antlers, a white-tailed doe, and two small fawns. It is a family. To me, deer are the trout of the forest, beautiful creatures, perfectly designed for their environs. Like a rainbow trout that swims with agility and grace, deer are thin, quick, and mobile, able to leap over branches and trunks, perfectly at home in their habitat.

Many consider deer a nuisance species. Friends who live outside the city often complain about the deer that invade and destroy their gardens and bushes. In some towns, there are deer hunts to cull the population. I find it strange to call a fellow creature of our planet, especially one that is so graceful, a nuisance.

I continue to look at the deer, and they stare back at me. There is a moment of silence, of harmony, as man and beast—both God's creatures—dwell together in peace. I think of the prophet Isaiah who taught that one day the animals of the land will not fear one another, that the wolf and the lamb will live together.

As I stand quietly in this moment with the deer, I think about my not-so-harmonious relationship with the trout of the stream. Most of the time, I am either trying to bring them to the net or quickly release them back into the river. Perhaps to assuage my feelings of guilt for disrupting the lives of the trout today, I will not break the peace of this moment with the deer. I stand still and breathe quietly. After a few moments, the doe turns her head toward her fawns as if to say: "Enough of this, let's get out of here." The doe hops into the woods, her white tail flopping, followed by the fawns. After one more good stare at me, the buck disappears after them.

A few minutes later, covered in sweat, I walk out of the woods. Before me I see the clubhouse and the sunset over the lake. The large orange sun is halfway down the horizon. The long, thin clouds near the horizon are painted purple and red. The surface of the lake forms a mirror image of all that is before me. It is as if I am seeing two sunsets. I feel doubly blessed. The lake is still, the insects are buzzing softly, and all the world is watching the end of the day.

I stop to watch the sun go down. I tell myself that I am not moving from this spot for a full five minutes. It is rare for me to sit still and just watch the world go by. I am always looking ahead, thinking about what I can accomplish in the next five minutes or five days or five years. It is so hard to live in the present, even if for just a little while.

When God first speaks to Abraham and Moses, they reply *hinaynee,* "here I am." They are present, their minds open and clear, ready to hear what God wishes to tell them. With the sunset before me, I put down my fishing rod and gear and sit, facing the lake. I turn my palms face up to help me open up within. I say *hinaynee,* here I am, ready to see this sunset, ready to hear the divine whispers in all that surrounds me.

As the minutes drift by, I realize that my day of fishing has taken me in a complete circle. I started in the south, at the shack and the park entrance. Then I headed west, sitting on the hard bench in front of the lake, watching the geese and swans swimming calmly in the noonday sun. My fishing journey took me far north, to the hatchery, and the source of the trout, and then later to beat number 7 where I held these magnificent creatures in my own hands. Now I am east, facing the lake and the clubhouse, watching the sun go down.

Sitting on the hard ground, I am starting to get antsy and hot. It's time to go home and shower. But I take one more minute to soak in the colors of the sunset, because today is not just a normal day of fly-fishing; it is one of my last trips on the Connetquot River. In a few months, I will leave New York City, where I have lived almost a decade, to move to Connecticut. I will head to a new home, a new temple, and I will search for new home waters as well.

The circle that I took around the lake today is like the circle of the journey of my last decade. I went from being a student to a teacher, an intern to a full-fledged rabbi ready for his own congregation. I am still the same person who came to New York City a decade ago, the same person who found his passion and love for Judaism and for trout streams. Yet in these ten years, I have learned from my teachers, my colleagues, and from many days fishing the riffles of these waters. I have been enriched and I have grown.

As the last sliver of the sun goes down below the horizon, I sit on the ground in front of the lake, in full fishing gear, hands and heart open. I think about my future in Connecticut, a place I only know from car trips from New York to Boston. I think about taking on my own congregation for the first time; I am excited and a bit nervous. The circle of the last decade has come to a close, and a new circle is beginning. I'll have to leave the Connetquot River soon and head for the Yankee north. But today is only April 3. Fly-fishing season is just beginning, and if I'm lucky, I can squeeze in a few more Monday trips to the Connetquot before I go.

## Reflection Questions

1.  Some days we catch a half dozen trout. On others we are skunked. What is success in fly-fishing? In life? How do we measure our own success and self-worth even if we do not catch the large trout or accomplish other goals that we set for ourselves?

2.  In what ways do you reflect at the end of a day of fly-fishing? What rituals help you bring an end to your day? What lessons do you learn from a day spent on the stream? How can you bring more opportunities for self-reflection into your life?

3.  The trip to the trout stream and the journey of our lives is a circle that is constantly renewed. When have you experienced endings and new beginnings in your life? When have you found potential, possibility, and new hope even in unexpected times or circumstances?

4.  How does time "flow" for you when you are doing things you love?

# Exercise: Five-Step Meditation for the End of the Day[1]

1. *Find your meditation spot.* This should be a private spot, free from external disturbances. You should feel safe, at peace, and comfortable in it.

2. *Sit in a comfortable position.* There are different recommendations on sitting positions, like the lotus position, sitting on a cushion, and so on. Find a position that's most comfortable for you. Whatever posture you choose, sit upright to facilitate the flow of energy.

3. *Clear your mind.* Loosen yourself up. Take a few deep, slow breaths, expanding your stomach as you breathe in, releasing your stomach as you exhale.

4. *Simply sit and observe.* Then, just sit back and observe the inner dialogue playing in your mind. What are you thinking? What are you feeling? Just observe; don't engage. Many people probably think that in meditation, they have to force themselves not to think and block out all their thoughts. It is really quite the opposite. You let your mind continue to think, but you don't engage. Meditate for as long as you want, until you feel cleansed, purified, refreshed, and ready to go.

5.  *Ending your meditation.* When you are done with your meditation, slowly ease into the physical state. Start off by being present to the physical reality around you. Next, be aware of your physical body. This can take fifteen to thirty seconds, or however long you need. Then, very slowly, open your eyes. Get attuned to your surroundings. Instead of resuming your physical activities immediately, you might want to continue sitting in the meditative spot and reflect upon some of the thoughts, feelings, or imagery that arose during your meditation. You may also want to just spend a few minutes expressing gratitude toward the things you enjoy in your life.

# CHAPTER FIVE

# COMMON GROUND

## FISHING WITH FRIENDS

*I have many loves and fly-fishing is one of them; it brings peace and harmony to my being, which I can then pass on to others.*

—*Sue Kreutzer, fly-fishing guide*

# RABBI ERIC: STREAM AND SPIRIT

One day in the spring I heard a knock on my office door at the temple in Connecticut. In comes a tall man wearing jeans, a button-down shirt, and a belt sporting a bronze trout on the buckle. He introduces himself as Bob and says he is looking for a rabbi to officiate at his upcoming wedding.

I invite Bob to sit, and he settles into my blue-and-yellow upholstered chair. I turn away from my endless streams of e-mails, push aside some papers on my desk, and listen.

Bob grew up in Fairfield, Connecticut, on the coast of Long Island Sound as a Christian. While working at the local hospital, Bob met Marina, who was born a

Jew in Russia. Marina's family came to New York City when she was young, settling in Sheepshead Bay at the bottom of Brooklyn, along with thousands of other Russian Jews. The practice of Judaism was outlawed in communist Russia, but many Jews there maintained their identity and the traditions and customs of the faith.

Bob explains that Marina wants a traditional Jewish wedding with a *chuppah* (marriage canopy), *ketubah* (the Jewish marriage license), and the breaking of the glass. Bob is open to a Jewish ceremony as well. The wedding will be followed by a Russian celebration of vodka and caviar at a nightclub in Sheepshead Bay. It's going to be some party, he says. I am intrigued.

I explain to Bob that many rabbis do not officiate at interfaith marriages. Yet I believe that an interfaith couple can make Jewish choices that will ensure the passing on of Judaism to the next generation. I tell Bob that I would be happy to officiate at his and Marina's wedding, and we arrange our next meeting to further discuss the ceremony.

Then I ask Bob about that belt buckle. Bob has been an angler since he was a kid, riding his bike to local streams and, later, chasing after big saltwater tuna and stripers (striped bass). Because of family and work obligations, he has not picked up a rod in a couple of years. We trade some stories about fishing the Housey and the Farmington in Connecticut. Bob clearly knows his stuff. I think to myself that we should go fishing together some time.

Two months later I am standing under the chuppah in our temple sanctuary. Bob is next to me, watching his bride walk down the aisle, a wide smile of joy upon his face. With Bob and Marina under the chuppah, I offer the traditional seven wedding blessings, and bride and groom sip from the wine cup. The Hebrew and English vows are spoken, and the rings are exchanged. At the end of the wedding ceremony Bob places a glass wrapped in a napkin on the floor and steps on it. This ritual symbolizes the loss of the Temple in Jerusalem, the fragility of life, and the break from the past as Bob and Marina become husband and wife. After the glass crunches under Bob's foot, we all say "Mazel tov!"

I turn to Bob and say that we will need this type of *mazel tov,* good luck, when we go fishing together next week. I cannot make the party at the Russian nightclub that night. Bob and I will celebrate his wedding in a different way, with a trip to the trout stream.

The following Monday, Bob picks me up in the early afternoon in his black two-seater car. We shake hands firmly, two men headed out on a trip. Bob's trunk is stuffed with fly-fishing gear. He spent all weekend checking his rods and organizing his flies. There is barely enough room for my green duffle and fly rod.

Today I left my St. Croix with the repaired reel seat at home and brought my Orvis rod instead. A few years ago, before our twins were born, my wife and I spent a long weekend in Manchester, Vermont, a beautiful tree-filled New England town known for its outlet shopping, skiing in the winter, and its place in fly-fishing history. Charles Orvis opened his first store there in 1856 on the banks of the Battenkill River, and, today, it is the flagship Orvis location.

While browsing the rack of fly rods at the Orvis store, I saw a back door. I went outside and found a tiny pond stocked with behemoth brownies and 'bows. Watching them swim around, slowly finning their massive weight through the water, got my heart pumping. A quarter mile from the Orvis store is the American Museum of Fly Fishing, where I saw the fly rods of Ernst Hemingway, Ted Williams, and President Dwight Eisenhower.

That day in Manchester, I purchased a seven-foot, 5-weight Orvis rod and reel. I use my St. Croix for the large Catskill Rivers and the wide Housey and Farmington in Connecticut. But I needed something smaller for the narrow streams of the Croton watershed that Bob and I will fish today.

Located fifty miles north of New York City, and only a half hour from where Bob and I live in Connecticut, the Croton streams have a long history that connect to New York City.

Since its beginning in the seventeenth century as the Dutch Colony of New Amsterdam, New York has always required drinking water for its burgeoning population. When local wells were not sufficient, The Collect Pond was dug on what is now Canal Street. After a nineteenth-century cholera epidemic, the residents of New York City began to tap the waters of the Croton River, where Bob and I are heading. The Croton Aqueduct was constructed to carry pure, cold water from the Croton River to Murray Hill in Manhattan in 1842. Today, the Croton watershed provides 10 percent of New York City's drinking water, with the rest coming from the Catskill Rivers further north. The rivers of the Croton watershed are a perfect habitat for trout: numerous dams were built to create reservoirs. Water that is released from the bottom of the dams is cold and pure year-round.

Bob shows me his watershed permit, a special license required to fish the watershed, which is a protected area because it still supplies drinking water. A half hour later we pull over near a tall dam, the beginning of the Amawalk River, which is named after a Native American tribe, as are many of the streams in this area.

When living in New York City, I mostly fished the Connetquot River on Long Island, as it was always filled with trout and located in a beautiful state park. I did make the occasional trip to the Croton watershed, but the fishing there was tough. The Croton rivers receive a lot of fishing pressure, with anglers coming from all over to cast a fly on the East and West Branch. My one trip to the Amawalk a few years ago yielded not a single bite. As we gear up, I share with Bob my previous fishless experience on this river. He says that today it's going to be different.

It is always a little strange to fish with someone for the first time. You never quite know how you will get along. If you don't, being on the stream with them will get old quickly. But Bob and I are both talkers, and I have a feeling we will be fine.

The Amawalk is a narrow stream winding through the forest, filled with naturally reproducing rainbows and browns that usually do not reach more than eight or ten inches. Bob tells me that this is his favorite type of stream, like the ones he grew up fishing. He would rather cast for smaller trout in a river that supports them year-round than a large river stocked with monster browns that cannot survive the hot summer. Fishing in natural trout waters just feels right to him.

Bob tells me that stealth is an often neglected but vital part of casting a fly. As we walk toward the first pool, Bob ducks down and instructs me to do the same. Wild fish, he says, are easily spooked, and the pool is small, flat, and smooth so that the fish could see us easily. We creep slowly and quietly toward the base of the pool.

I watch Bob step gently into the water and I follow. The pool seems too shallow, and I cannot imagine that it holds any fish at all. Bob hands me a tiny brown mayfly that he tied himself. I attach it to my leader and begin to cast twenty feet or so upstream. I feel a little self-conscious about my casting at first. Then I begin to relax and sink into the rhythm of the cast and the swishing sound of the line flying through the air. Bob suggests various places in the pool and offers me another fly when I lose mine to a tree branch. I hook a small, wild brownie and we both smile.

Since I officiated at his wedding, I am Bob's rabbi. The word *rabbi* means teacher. But as I cast in the stream with Bob looking on, I am a student, learning from someone whose knowledge of trout and flies far exceeds mine. If I am Bob's rabbi, he is my teacher of all things trout.

We fish up and down the Amawalk for a few hours, sometimes together and other times alone. Bob and I each hook a few small wild trout and a number of tiny smallmouth bass that share the stream with the salmonids.

The sun has gone down and it is now dark. Bob reaches into his vest and pulls out a small LED hiking light on a strap. He wraps the light around his head, turns it on and a bright beam shines onto the leafy path, showing the way with ease. "Pretty handy," he says. Bob then turns his head toward the stream, and the light follows. The surface of the river is illuminated and we see bugs swimming, flying, and swarming.

As we watch the tiny insects, I am reminded of the story of Creation from the Bible. God said, "Let the waters bring forth swarms of living creatures," like the bugs Bob and I see before us on the stream. Bob points out various insects and their Latin names, all of which are new to me. I think about Adam in the Garden of Eden, who gave names to all of the animals and the birds of the sky. With trout and swarming bugs and Latin names, Bob and I are reliving the story of Creation.

At the end of the sixth day, God surveys all that He has made and calls it *tov meod,* very good. With the light of his LED hiking lamp, Bob and I stand in a river. We watch the bugs and talk about the trout we held in our hands that day. At that moment, I realize that the world is very good, indeed.

After a few more moments on the stream, Bob and I traipse through the darkness back to his car. Avoiding the traffic that is whizzing by on Route 35, we strip off our waders, put away our rods, and head home.

Two weeks later, Bob pulls up to my house in his black car with two passengers, his sons Bobby and Jay. At fourteen, Bobby is starting to enjoy fly-fishing, riding his bike to local streams like his father used to do when he was young, and spending hours casting for small brookies and brownies. Bobby's younger brother Jay is ten and can cast just fine. The trip to the Farmington River is an hour and a half from home. Bobby sleeps and listens to his iPod like a normal teenager. Jay jabbers on, asking all sorts of questions about fishing, the sites we pass by, and anything else that comes into his young mind, all of which Bob does his best to answer.

As we make our way to the stream, I remember being Jay's age and going fishing with my own father in St. Louis. Before dawn, we packed the car, a 1980s Cadillac Seville, with our Zebco bass rods, and traditional ball-shaped plastic bobbers, half red and half white. Like Bob's younger son, in my excitement to go fishing I used to talk nonstop as we drove with the rising sun. Finally, my dad and I arrived at Busch's Wildlife, named for the founders of the Anheuser-Busch brewery, a St. Louis institution. The nature preserve contained a few dozen small bass and bluegill lakes.

At the state park building, we chose our lake. Unlike my trips to the Connetquot River on Long Island two decades later, we did not have to wait in line or pay to fish at Busch's Wildlife. My dad and I always picked a lake that was not too populated with other anglers. At the tackle shop we purchased the requisite night crawlers, large earthworms that looked like they were on steroids, to thread onto three-pronged hooks.

Together my dad and I would sit on the dock and watch the red-and-white bobber on the smooth surface of the lake. After a little while, the bobber would disappear, and I'd jerk up the rod in excitement and yell. My dad said: "Take it easy or you'll yank the hook out of the fish's mouth." After a well-fought battle between a ten-year-old not yet fly-fishing rabbi and an invisible fish at the end of the line, I pulled up a six-inch smallmouth bass. Sometimes we took one home and fried it up with flour and salt. The tiny bass would only yield a few bites and lots of bones, but it was always more about the thrill of catching than the size of the fish.

My dad was never much of a fisherman himself, but he would take me to Busch's Wildlife because he knew that I loved it. We sat on the dock together and talked about the St. Louis Cardinals, about school, and about whatever came into my head. Those father and son days on the bass lakes were special times in my childhood. I take these memories of my dad and me fishing with me each time I put on my waders and cast a fly.

Back on the Farmington River in Connecticut, I hope that this day will be as special for Bob and his sons. We will be fishing a part of the river next to the ball field. It is late afternoon and we hear the metallic sound of an aluminum bat striking the ball, and the cheers of the crowd at the Little League game. Bob brought along sliced turkey, bread, and cheese, and we eat our sandwiches standing next to the open trunk of the car.

Today we will fish a wide smooth stretch of stream in the Farmington, easy enough for the boys to get around. The Farmington is another reservoir-fed river that remains cold year-round, even in the dog days of summer. I always enjoy the freezing water of the Farmington as the sun goes down on an August evening.

As we gear up, Bob is busy being a father, helping his sons get their flies tied on and waders snug. He gives me a look as if to say, *it's much easier when it's just the two of us.* I think about my twin children who are less than two years old. It is so much work just to get them out of the house, much less go on a big adventure like a fishing trip.

Finally we are all in the river. Bob and his sons fish together. I wade across the stream to the opposite shore. I alternate between casting and watching the others fish. Bob helps Jay get his fly free from the bushes a few times. Then Jay gets his first strike and lets out a high screeching yell. Bob tells Jay to take it easy, just like my dad told me, and like all fathers tell their excited sons and daughters who have a fish on the line.

Jay pulls out a small brownie, not much bigger than the six-inch bass I caught years ago with my dad. After Bob helps him release the trout, Jay is all smiles. Then, right there on the stream, Jay recounts the story with great excitement in his squeaky ten-year-old prepubescent voice.

On the opposite shore of the river, and of my own life, I listen to Jay ramble on. I was once a ten-year-old fishing the bass lakes of Missouri with my dad. Now I am a father myself. One day in the not-too-distant future, I will take my own children to the trout stream. I will help them tie on their flies, and smile as I listen to their squeals as they hook their first trout.

After a few hours on the Farmington and a couple of brown trout brought to the net, it's time to head home. We arrive back in Ridgefield well after dark. I say goodbye to the boys. Bob and I make plans for our next fishing trip to the Housey in a couple of weeks. We shake hands. From a knock on my office door at the temple and a conversation about a trout belt buckle, to officiating at Bob's wedding, and then fishing the streams of New York and Connecticut, we have both been enriched by our friendship. As I watch the car drive away, I realize that Bob and I are now fishing buddies who will share many more adventures together on the stream.

# REVEREND MIKE: FISHING INTO THE MYSTERY

One thing humans share is a dual need for community and solitude. We function best when we tend to both. In our modern, hectic world, we rarely nurture and develop community and solitude in loving, creative, and healthy ways.

We have instant "friends" via social networks. We text, tweet, and e-mail instantly. While these phenomena certainly enable us to cast our nets wide, they do not fill the places in our hearts and souls provided by deep encounters with humans who love, understand, and care for us.

True community breaks down walls, encourages human growth and potential, and provides a safety zone when we are broken and hurt. True community like that is increasingly rare in our world. Often, churches and synagogues are starting points that can foster the kind of radical trust that true community can provide.

Paradoxically, we also seem to need periods of solitude. We need time alone to listen to our hearts, interpret our needs, understand the role we play in creation, allow ourselves to heal from the toils of the world, and renew our spirits. Again, modern life doesn't encourage true silence and solitude. We are victims of noise pollution and sensory overload. We are always "doing" when we need more "being." We need to be still, to rest our weary bones, and to step out of all of the many demands that life places on us.

Balance seems to be the key here—finding a healthy balance between community and solitude is something all spiritual giants have taken seriously. Saint Benedict, the founder of the monastic movement that swept Christianity in the fourth century, knew that intuitively. Deliberate tending to both of those human needs is one of the foundations for a healthy, whole, creative life.

No activity that I know of satisfies both of these needs as well as fly-fishing does. Good trips are most often taken with longstanding, close friends who share a love of this sport. On these trips, we not only share travel and the time on the water together, we solve all of the world's problems at night after the mandatory fishing stories are told.

There is a ritual pattern to every trip I have taken. We fish hard all day. We spend time on the river dealing with inner issues, while solving the technical issues of the fish and what they are feeding on. Then we return to the cabin or lodge.

There, the barriers come down amid the telling of stories and the sharing of our inner lives. We talk not only about fishing, but children, work, politics, longings, desires, dreams lost and found. We have drinks and smoke post-dinner cigars as the evening draws to a close. We gaze at the stars and moon, and sit in silent awe at the glory of creation.

There may be periods of silence and reflection. Listening is just as important as talking, and I've found anglers to be among the best listeners. We tend to take our lives seriously and yet with humor and joy, so the periods of time back at the cabin are among life's richest treasures.

My brother-in-law, David, was my roommate in medical school and later married my sister. He remains my best friend, and we talk on the phone almost weekly, even though we have never practiced medicine in the same community. We share a love of fishing, literature, music, and writing. At the same time I was exploring my spiritual vocation by attending an Episcopal seminary, he was getting a master's in creative writing in Vermont.

Like me, he seems to find himself caught in the tension between his science background and gifts (he is an oncologist) and his love of writing and fishing. He was taught how to fish at an early age by his grandfather. Today, he is the best angler I've ever seen, bar none. He has an innate "fish sense" that is almost spooky, and his technique is superb. But he has an even greater skill that sets him apart from most of us. He reads water like the blood that runs through his veins. He senses when fish are there and when they are not. He sees the rise and take better than most. And finally, even after fishing all of his life, he is like a little kid on the river. It brings him the deep, raw, pure joy of being alive and full of a grateful heart for this gift of fishing we have been given.

Being raised Catholic in west Texas must have been no easy matter in those early days, but David's grandfather always taught him that he simply must spend all of Good Friday in the water fly-fishing. So even though that was not a holiday in the public schools, David always took the day off to fish with his grandfather. His grandfather claimed that since that was the day Christ's blood was spilled, the earth was contaminated. Therefore, it was mandatory to spend as much of that day as possible wading in the waters of the earth instead of walking on desecrated land. The stories we pass on to justify our time on the river never cease to amaze me!

A decade or so ago, David and I fished in Tierra del Fuego in Argentina, at the southernmost point of South America, for the famous sea-run brown trout. Our guide, a gregarious, bilingual, funny guy named Ozzie, was a gifted storyteller. And tell them Ozzie did. Story after story of funny clients, quirks of the river, great wine, food, and loves he has shared.

He had an insatiable appetite for American music and was quite knowledgeable about rock-and-roll. This was in the early days of the iPod craze, so when we returned home, my brother-in-law and I bought Ozzie an iPod, loaded it up with great music, and shipped it to him in Argentina! Even today we hear from him regularly, as music and the love of fishing has forged, yet again, one more community that sustains us.

There is nothing that makes me happier than fishing with women and seeing the pure joy they experience when they get in tune with what is going on. I had invited my friend Steve and his wife Candy to our place in Colorado to play in the member/guest golf tournament. Steve loves golf, but he loves having a rod in his hand perhaps even more. Like me, he responds at some deep level to rivers, and I see the joy and focus that he brings to his time in the water.

Candy has put up with Steve teaching her to fly-fish and has developed a beautiful, technically lovely cast of her own. But freshwater trout fishing is a bit new to both of them, and Steve has fallen in love with the Frying Pan River. He is particularly fond of one of my favorite stretches—the Eagle's Nest Pool. It is the perfect place for couples. The wading is generally easy, it is hidden from the road, and there are several grassy banks where you can sit and rest and watch your friends work to rising fish. It is a nice place to spend an evening, sip wine, talk, and see lots of fish.

And that's where Steve and I and our wives, Candy and Gail, ended up late one summer afternoon. We walked into the water around 6:00p.m. and were greeted with the sight of hundreds of fish rising to an evening pale morning dun hatch. The four of us waded in.

There were plenty of fish, and we caught a steady stream of nice thirteen- to sixteen-inch fish in water that is very easy to read and see the take. But I could tell Steve was chomping at the bit to really work a slot he knew about upstream and to the right. I told Steve I would fish with Candy a while, and Gail stepped out quietly and found her favorite spot to rest.

There is a spot about a hundred yards upstream and to the left of the main fishing zone. As light dims, it is hard to see up there. The light changes and at first the glare is right where you need to be watching your fly land in a hole right below a little riffle that you don't see until you are right on it. I know it often holds the rare, huge rainbow and even a few large cutbow trout. They don't get fished to very often this time of day, but when the patient angler works up there quietly, he or she is often rewarded.

Candy and I took our time—I wanted to arrive just as it got too dark to tie a fly on without my Orvis headlamp. I also made sure I had a few no-hackle PMDs handy, my favorite fly for late evening, as they seem to dance on the surface in such a lovely, lifelike way. They are a bit hard to fish, since they get wet and sink easily, so you have to use plenty of desiccant to keep the fly visible and floating high, but they do catch fish.

Candy and I worked quietly and steadily up the slot along the willows to the left bank of the river. She caught five or six nice fish and was really getting into the zone—seeing the fish take, presenting the fly in the seam perfectly, and working them to the side where I could get them in the net quickly without stressing them.

But my heart was beginning to race, as I knew we were only about fifteen yards away from the magic spot. I stopped our upstream walk and turned on my headlamp in order to tie on a new, perfectly dry no-hackle. I pointed out the rock and the slot just downstream of it where Candy needed to present the fly.

It was almost too dark to see, but, once her vision settled down, she saw what I was seeing. I had her keep her polarized glasses on. Even though it was too dark to see into the water, I believe wearing them helped her to pick up the fly quicker. We waded within about twenty feet of the landing zone. I gave her fly a few good shakes of dessicant, and told her to lay the line five feet below the rock we could barely see, and cautioned her to be ready when the fly hit the water. If there was a fish there, it wouldn't play around. It would inhale the fly and move to the fast water in the middle. She wouldn't get a second chance at it.

Candy took a breath, held the fly in her left hand gently, made one perfect back cast, and released it forward. As if in slow motion, the fly landed exactly where we wanted, and in an explosion of color and sound, water droplets erupted. A huge rainbow had nailed the fly, and leapt free of the water before returning to it and muscling its way for the strong, deep current in the middle.

Like a Zen master, Candy held the rod high and pointed it to the bank, effectively turning the fish from its run and toward my gently waiting net. It was all so fast and low stress that the nineteen-inch rainbow allowed Candy to cradle it gently in her hands while I took the mandatory picture. If I have ever seen a more happy, satisfied, and content angler I cannot remember it!

One of my goals in fishing is to try to learn something new each trip, and, of course, there is always something new to learn, no matter how many years we participate in this beautiful sport. It is so very much like life; always changing and shifting and flowing. As I reflected on that time with Candy, I knew enough about her to know that she is a very spirit-filled person. She takes her faith journey seriously, meditates, and practices centering prayer faithfully. She has a core stillness that is hard to describe but is very visible in her serenity and equanimity. This translates into the perfect set of inner and outer gifts and skills that "work" on the river.

Most people at her level of technical skill would have hardly been able to contain themselves, but as we moved into the zone, she moved slower, not faster. She read the water, the light, the fish, and the ethos of the moment. When we release our emotional "stuff," let go of our unceasing demands and our minds, find our spiritual center, and live fully in the presence of the moment, we experience the indescribable magic that Candy found at the Eagle's Nest Pool.

# Reflection Questions

1. What do you enjoy about fishing with others? What are the benefits of casting a fly by yourself? How has participation in communities shaped your inner journey? How has solitude done the same?

2. What are your earliest fishing memories? Who took you fishing when you were young, and what do you remember from the experience? In what ways does fishing connect the generations, grandparents, parents, and children?

3. When have you been a student of fly-fishing, and who taught you? When have you been a teacher to others on the stream? Whom do you seek out to learn spiritual and religious truths? What have you shared with others from your inner journey?

# Exercise: Become a Part of a Fly-Fishing Community

From sharing tips and good fishing spots on the local river to telling stories of the monster brown that got away, being a part of a group of like-minded anglers enriches the experience of fly-fishing.

Two national organizations, Trout Unlimited (www.tu.org) and the Federation of Fly Fishers (www.fedflyfishers.org) organize local chapters in which anglers meet to discuss trout, conservation, and all things fly-fishing.

Online fly-fishing forums also bring anglers together to share their fishing tips and stories on the web. For some of our favorites, see the "Fly-Fishing Resources" section at the back of this book.

CHAPTER SIX

# UNFAMILIAR TERRAIN

## FISHING FAR FROM HOME

*One day, I left in a straight line from my home at 41 Kachele Street, east along the 41st parallel, following my passion for fish. It was a journey not only away from home, but toward it; which is the beauty of traveling in a circle and the irony of adventure.*

—James Prosek, American artist, writer, and naturalist

# REVEREND MIKE: FISHING INTO THE MYSTERY

In chapter two, I sang praises to the familiarity of place. In many ways, that familiarity is also very much a part of our religious lives. Our prayers and acts, instead of being repetitive and stale, become living ways of encountering the holy in a known rhythm.

For Christians, the four-part action that we call Holy Communion has that mysterious power we call *anamnesis.* Anamnesis can be thought of as a living memory—not a recitation of a dark relic of the past but an act that brings memory of an event in the past to the present. It is a reenactment of the Last Supper that Christ shared with his disciples, but it is done in a way that Christians believe makes the shared meal holy and living in their lives. It is a transcendent moment and event that is beyond rationality, language, or empiric verification. It is not "magic" at all, but a way of encountering a God who exists both within and beyond the boundaries of time.

When we "take" Communion, we bless the host, we break it into pieces for the gathered community, and we share it. The pieces become a part of our brokenness that is healed when we bring them back to God. We celebrate our lives with bread and water—indeed the stuff of life itself. When asked what to pray for, Jesus was very specific. Give us this bread that we need for the day. No more, no less. Strength to sustain us for the journey.

But, there comes a time when we are called to depart from familiar territory and go to distant waters. Like Abraham, we are called to respond, to leave what is known and comfortable. Getting out of our comfort zones is the hardest thing any of us are ever called to do. We leave behind known waters and depart for distant lands. We leave the rhythms of fish and streams that we know like the backs of our hands and attempt to test our skills against a totally new environment. It is simultaneously liberating and daunting.

For we can easily become creatures of habit, and if we are fortunate enough to be able to fish known waters much of the time, it is far too easy to get stuck there. We don't push ourselves emotionally, spiritually, or intellectually. And while the time spent in home waters is never "wasted," I believe we all long for a time when we can move into new territories. We long for new challenges, new opportunities, new ways of experiencing the nuances of water and fish.

For me, this has involved quite a bit of travel over the years. I have fished the waters of New Zealand, South America, the Caribbean, Belize, and Alaska. Each trip represents a new beginning for me, for I have to get out my books and guides and leave my comfort zone. I have to learn new flies, new gear, new insects. I have to get out my large rods, which feel so different from the featherweight rods I use in my home waters.

A month or two before these trips, I bring out the 10/12-weight and practice my heavy-rod casting. I begin to work on the double-haul, something we don't have to do in the Rockies. I try to get my muscle memory back in shape, so that I don't waste a part of a trip having to relearn things that I don't get to practice often enough.

Our spiritual lives often need the same sort of jump-starting. We need to challenge ourselves to take on new disciplines, new ideas, and new ways of exploring our connection to God. For me, this willingness to try new things has led me to sudden spurts of feeling a connection to God, as well as to new waters. They seem to go hand in hand. But as Abraham discovered when he left his home for a new land, it can only happen when we say, yes.

Several years ago, I was sitting in the Houston Intercontinental Airport when my cell phone rang. It was the wife of Will Spong, the man who was perhaps my closest mentor in my dual life as a physician and priest. Will was my seminary professor, pastoral counselor, and one of my closest friends. He was found dead in bed that morning, and my world began to spin out of control.

Will was the brother of the Reverend John Shelby Spong, who wrote *Rescuing the Bible from Fundamentalists,* and was the person most responsible for my decision to pursue ordained ministry while continuing a life as a practicing physician and professor. We had just shared a long lunch a few weeks before; little did I know then that would be the last time I would see him.

When Nancy called to inform me of Will's passing, I was on the way to Argentina to pursue the legendary sea-run brown trout of Tierra del Fuego. I wanted desperately to cancel the trip to be with Will's friends and family, to celebrate his life and ministry. Yet Nancy told me unequivocally to go fishing—that is what Will would have wanted for me. So, I went fly-fishing—to the land of eternal fire where large fish morphed into something glorious to rule the rivers and oceans.

Two days later, I was in the middle of the Rio Grande when the reality of Will's death hit me. I began to heave with sobs of loss, of injustice, of Will's pure and simple absence. I went to the bank to collect myself, fearing that if I stayed in the water I might lose my balance and go for a cold swim! Within a few minutes I began to feel a peace, a calm—what I would describe as a peace that passes all understanding.

I looked across the river, and my eyes beheld the most glorious rainbow that I've ever seen. Now, this was more than a bit unusual, for it was not an arched rainbow reaching from cloud to cloud, but a vertical rainbow reaching from heaven to earth, like a multicolored thread reaching from the Divine into the heart of the human condition.

And I heard, with the clarity beyond words, Will's voice inside my head saying "Mike, it is fine. All will be well. Relax and don't worry." The words of the fourteenth-century Christian mystic Julian of Norwich echoed in my mind—when she looked into a simple chestnut and saw all of God's creation and wrote "all will be well, all will be well." It was nothing less than the simple assurance of the presence of creating God who undergirds His story with an outpouring of love into the human condition.

The Celtic Christians of the first few centuries felt that the world is graced with "thin places," where the Divine and human can more closely come into some sort of connection with each other. These are "liminal" places, and they exist in all sorts of strange and wonderful and glorious spots. Sometimes they are in churches or temples or synagogues. Sometimes they are in the fields we plow. Sometimes they are in our kitchen or our hearth, where we are welcomed home. More often, they are in the world where we all live daily.

These are places where we experience the reality of God more purely, more certainly, more radically, more authentically than in other places. And, for me, rivers are often those very thin places. Like the river in Argentina, they are often places where my mind and body can get out of the way, and God can flow in. Unobstructed with the clutter of my life, I find myself listening more intently to the voice that is calling me home, to the very ground of my being.

# RABBI ERIC: STREAM AND SPIRIT

At 6:00a.m. on a Tuesday in December, I am standing on the front patio of my mother-in-law's house in Alta Gracia, Argentina, waiting for my fly-fishing guide, Lucas, to pick me up.

Alta Gracia is a small town of 50,000 people, an hour's drive from Cordoba, the second largest city in Argentina. In the late nineteenth and early twentieth centuries, millions of Jews left eastern Europe and Russia to escape anti-Jewish pogroms and violence. The vast majority came to the United States, and over a million settled on the Lower East Side of Manhattan.

My family went farther west to St. Louis, a thriving industrial city on the Mississippi at the time. My wife's family headed to Argentina; I like to say that after leaving Europe, they took a left, heading south to join a thriving community of 150,000 of their fellow Jews in Argentina. My wife's grandfather founded a textile factory in Alta Gracia that manufactures classic Argentinean ponchos for the gauchos, the cowboys that tend the cattle that become the steak and beef for which the country is known.

As I stand on the porch in Alta Gracia, I breathe in the warm December air. While my friends and family are trudging through the snow of a typical Connecticut winter, December is the middle of the summer in the Southern Hemisphere.

I look down and see my trusty green fishing bag and my four-piece St. Croix rod in its hard canvas case, the same gear that I brought on countless trips to the Connetquot River on Long Island and then, later, to the Farmington and Housey in Connecticut. Now, I hope that my rod will help me land some large trout on the streams of central Argentina.

When traveling with my fly-fishing gear, I always check the duffle with my luggage, as the assorted hooks and sharp objects would never make it through security. But the rod is a different story. This is my St. Croix 5/6-weight rod, the one I bought as a teenager and that I repaired myself when the reel seat broke. If this rod got lost or damaged among the heavy suitcases under the plane, I would be bereft. So I always bring my fly rod on the plane and put it right next to my seat, just for safe-keeping. The twenty-four-inch cylindrical case never quite fits in an airplane chair, jutting out and pushing against my elbow.

Along with my fly-fishing gear, my wife and I also brought our twin eight-month-old babies on this trip to Argentina. It was a full twenty-four hours from the moment we left home in Connecticut until arriving at my mother-in-law's house in Alta Gracia, a day of washing bottles in airport bathrooms, making formula at 35,000 feet, and trying not so successfully to sleep in a cramped airline seat with a baby on each of our laps. I managed to convince my wife that since we were bringing our daughter and son down to visit her family, just maybe I could sneak away for three days of fly-fishing. Somehow she agreed.

Now, at 6:00a.m., as the babies sleep back in the house, I see Lucas pull up in his pickup truck, a worn gray Toyota. As we load my bag into the cab, I recall my good fortune in finding a fly-fishing guide in Argentina who speaks English.

I first met Lucas on a trout stream here three years previously. During that visit, my mother-in-law mentioned that she heard about a good local river to fish. The next day, we headed out of Alta Gracia and drove through the grassy hills and steppes. After an hour, we descended into a valley. A hundred feet ahead on the road, I saw a tiny bridge that crossed thirty feet or so of river, its stones submerged by the stream. As we drove across it, our tires were a few inches underwater.

We had arrived at the Rio San Jose. The bridge that we had just crossed served as a dam, forming a long smooth pool upstream, one that I hoped was filled with trout. Then I saw the first rise, a tiny splash in the mirror-flat pool.

As I ran my green fly line through the guides on the rod, I heard what sounded like a loud stomping noise. It began to get louder. I looked up to see a herd of cows coming down the gravel road, toward the bridge. In front and back were two gauchos on horseback. A few dogs ran up and down with the herd as the cows made their way across the bridge.

As I watched this procession of man and beast, I found myself thinking of Psalm 23, The Lord is my shepherd. Seeing the gauchos guiding the cows, I stopped and offered thanks for arriving at such a unique place so far from my home.

When the herd finished crossing the bridge, I walked toward the pool. At the edge of the stream I saw a sign: Cordoba Trucha Club. Even with my rudimentary Spanish skills, I knew that this was the Cordoba Trout Club. My wife translated the rest of the sign for me, which described how the San Jose River was under the care of the club, that all of the rainbow trout in the water were naturally reproducing, and that only fly-fishing with artificial lures was permitted. Even though I was three thousand miles from Connecticut, seeing that sign made me feel at home in a trout stream that my fellow anglers cared for and protected.

The fish in the mirror-smooth pool were obviously well-acquainted with anglers. While I sent numerous flies up and down the stream, not a single fish would bite, even though they kept rising. A few minutes later, I saw another angler, an Argentinean man about my age, thin, with tanned skin and decked out in full fly-fishing gear.

He came up and introduced himself in English as Lucas, one of the leaders of the Cordoba Trucha Club. He told me about their work to preserve and protect the Rio San Jose. Lucas suggested I tie on a longer tippet, because in the clear smooth water the fish could see the thicker line of the leader. We fished together for a while on that pool, without any luck. Lucas mentioned that he was also a guide and would be happy to take me out fishing. I told him that that sounded great, but I was leaving Argentina the next day. So we traded e-mails, shook hands, and I reeled in.

Three years later, Lucas and I are now driving in his truck, gear loaded, embarking on a three-day fly-fishing trip together. This is my first time away from our twins since they were born, and it feels a bit strange to not have to worry about bottles or diapers. As the road drifts by, I realize that I am headed out for three days with a more or less complete stranger in a country where I do not speak the language. I hope that Lucas will guide me well, to streams filled with trout and adventure. If the Lord is my shepherd, for the next three days I am counting on Lucas to be my fishing guide.

Our first stop is the Rio San Jose. This time, three years later, we are going to explore other more remote parts of the stream. At 7:30a.m., Lucas parks the truck in front of a wooden gate. There is not a soul around for miles. The rolling grassy hills stretch out in all directions, crisscrossed by the barbed wire fences that mark the boundaries of the many cattle ranches. We begin the hike down to the stream, avoiding the cow patties that dot the road.

In this section, the Rio San Jose flows through a gorge. We gear up, and Lucas trots out ahead, down the rocks and toward the stream. A minute later he is well ahead of me. I am stepping carefully from rock to rock, thinking that a sprained ankle would ruin my fly-fishing trip in a hurry, while Lucas is almost jogging across the boulders.

Watching Lucas maneuver through the rocks reminds me of another agile creature that I once saw. While living in Jerusalem and studying to become a rabbi, I took a trip to the Sinai Peninsula. I spent the night at Saint Catherine's monastery at the foot of Mount Sinai. At 4:00a.m., I awoke and got on a camel, a strange and smelly creature that lazily took me up a winding path for over an hour. At the top of Mount Sinai, shivering in the wind, I and a dozen other tourists watched the sun rise, the sharp peaks all around coming to life in pink, purple, and orange. While historically we cannot be sure that this is the actual Mount Sinai, I understood that day how Moses could have felt God's presence in such a glorious place.

While the camel takes you up Mount Sinai, you walk down yourself. As I made my way back down, I stared at the jutting peaks that surrounded me. I glanced across at another mountain, and I saw something moving on a tiny ledge, at least a quarter mile away. It was a goat, eating the leaves of a tiny shrub. I marveled at the ingenuity of this animal and its ability to survive in such a barren place. After a few seconds, the mountain goat skipped away gracefully behind the rocks.

Back in Argentina, as I watch Lucas trot across the rocks of the Rio San Jose, I remember that goat on Mount Sinai. I yell to Lucas to slow down. I tell him that he looks like a mountain goat out here, leaping from rock to rock with such ease. We both smile.

The Rio San Jose is a medium-sized stream filled with rainbow trout that were first stocked decades ago but now reproduce naturally. I start out fishing a Griffith's Gnat, a black fly with white bristling threads. After a bit, I change to my favorite brown Elk-Hair Caddis, the same fly that always makes the fish of the Connetquot River of Long Island and the streams of Connecticut rise. I catch a few small 'bows and release them back to their home.

Lucas and I leave the pool and begin to hike, following the terrain as the cliffs rise well above the stream. After a few moments, we are standing on the edge of the rocks, looking down a good fifty feet at a deep pool with riffles at each end. Lucas stops and tells me to cast into the pool, that there are many good trout down there.

I have never cast down a cliff into a river before. Lucas instructs me to tilt my fly rod forward, so that the casting plane will point down. I stand on the edge of the cliff and begin to false cast, the fly sailing past my head, well up into the sky, and then down the cliff face toward the pool.

As the fly glides through the air, I feel a little like Zeus casting a lightning bolt from the sky. I feel like I am again on Mount Sinai, on top of the world. I take a few extra casts to soak in the moment, and then let the fly land at the edge of the pool. It floats for a second, and then I hear a clap; a fish is on. Following the lead of my mountain-goat guide, we make our way down the cliff, somehow keeping the fish on the line, and I bring a fourteen-inch rainbow trout to the net. Holding that fish in my hands, I feel like I am at the peak of all creation.

We spend a few more hours on the Rio San Jose, and then it is time to head to our next destination. Lucas and I load up the truck and sit and drink a beer on the river bank. The first day of our trip was a great success; we caught a few 'bows on the Rio San Jose, and I learned to cast from the sky.

By the time we leave the Rio San Jose, it is well into the afternoon. I snack on dried fruit and bread as we speed down the highway. Soon the road begins to climb. A large mountain stretches out before us.

As we approach that mountain in Argentina, I remember a driving trip I took with friends as a teenager. We left from my hometown of St. Louis for my friend's cabin in Colorado, driving all night through the flat cornfields of Missouri and Kansas in shifts of three hours. I volunteered for the 4:00 to 7:00a.m. shift, since I am energetic in the mornings.

The first two hours seemed to stretch out to infinity. But then I saw the first light of dawn, the sun rising behind us as we headed west on Interstate 70. I woke up my friends. And then, as if on cue, there was enough light in the sky to illuminate the Rocky Mountains. We had been driving all night through the flattest country God had ever made. Then, just when the sun rose, the mountains came into view, and we greeted a new and glorious day.

As Lucas and I keep driving, we find ourselves crossing a long, wide plateau. The top of this mountain is flat. Lucas points out a national park in which hikers battle snow and ice in the winter. Antennas jut up from the small ranger station at the entrance to the park, their reception unimpeded at this height. Like casting my fly from the cliffs of the Rio San Jose, I once again feel on top of the world. I am grateful to Lucas for bringing me here.

As we descend the mountain, it has gotten dark and Lucas and I are driving on a one-lane road with no streetlights. Only the occasional headlights approaching us in the opposite direction remind me that we are not totally alone.

As we drive through the dark, our conversation begins to wander from flies and fishing techniques to other more spiritual matters. Lucas asks me if I believe in UFOs (I am not so sure). We speak about the power of religion to both strengthen and be destructive. I realize that he and I have more in common than just a love of trout. Lucas is a Catholic, Spanish-speaking Argentinean, while I am a Connecticut Reform rabbi, but we both seek to understand our world and our place within it.

An hour later we are driving through a dark valley. We take a right turn, and I see a single light shining ahead, like a distant lighthouse as seen from the sea.

Lucas tells me that this is our hotel, a rural stop-off built for tourists on a local lake. As we approach that single light, I feel the isolation of this place. Here I am in the middle of rural Argentina with a fly-fishing guide I barely know, in complete darkness, with only a single light to guide us. I pause to appreciate the simplicity and oneness of this moment.

Lucas and I check into the hotel and sit down for a late meal. Argentineans never eat before 8:00, with 10:00p.m. being the usual dinner hour. Lucas recommends the fish, which turns out to be a bony white fillet; no trout on this menu. As we eat, Lucas tells me of his adventures in Patagonia, and how, the next time I come down, he will take me there. Lucas says that I have to learn the double-haul, a cast in which an extra pull upon the line during the casting motion produces much greater distance. Easier said than done! As we chat over dessert, Lucas and I are becoming friends.

The next morning, after a traditional Argentinean breakfast of coffee and toast with butter and *dulce de leche,* we head for the stream. Today, Lucas and I will fish the Rio Quines, private waters that flow through a cattle ranch. Lucas knows the owner and already spoke to him. We pull off the highway onto a dirt road that you would only find if you knew where to look. Lucas puts the truck in low gear, and we move along at ten miles an hour over large rocks and through holes. We park next to a small stone cabin with no door that was abandoned long ago. Lucas and

I begin the hike down to the stream. We find ourselves in a gorge, and, once again, I struggle to keep up with him.

Lucas tells me that we will use Woolly Buggers on a sinking fly line. A majority of the time in Connecticut, I fish dry flies on the surface and nymphs below. While the Woolly Bugger is a popular fly, I have never used it before. Lucas says that today is the time to learn something new. The word "rabbi" means teacher. Every week I give sermons and teach classes for children and adults. Today with Lucas, I will be the student.

We wade into the stream and I begin to roll cast the black Woolly Bugger. Lucas shows me how to swing the fly across the stream and then pull it in slowly. Stripping in the line makes the Woolly Bugger swim like the tiny minnow that it is supposed to imitate. We work the pools and currents, Lucas not letting me cast more than two or three times at a spot, always pointing to the next pool, as he says again and again "Strip, strip, strip the line."

As I keep casting, I am finding it hard to take so much direction. In other areas of my life, I value learning, whether as a student in college or for five years of rabbinical school. I know that learning from others makes you a better person.

But something about fly-fishing is different. I taught myself to cast on my St. Croix rod that I bought in St. Louis. I caught my first trout without ever having a fly-fishing lesson and knowing next to nothing about flies and bugs. Over the years, I have learned from many friends and guides, including Bob, my Connecticut friend who somehow can sneak up on an eight-inch wild brookie in a crystal clear pool. Yet I still recoil from too much instruction when I am on the stream.

Fly-fishing is often a do-it-yourself endeavor, a way of being as close to nature as humanly possible, to rekindle the hunting genes within us that are so often buried in a world of computer screens and e-mails. I want to live that fantasy of being the primal fly-fisher on the stream, alone and capable, hooking trout all day long. I want to be the David that slays the Goliath trout with only my wits and a fly line in place of a slingshot. Or maybe I just like doing some things myself.

Lucas continues to give me instruction, and I ignore my ego. As the hours pass, I listen and practice, and my technique improves. I hook my first trout on a black Woolly Bugger, a nice size rainbow that I release into the stream.

We fish the Rio Quines all afternoon, alternating between Woolly Buggers and various dry flies, bringing a few trout to the net here and there. I return to the hotel exhausted and sleep well that night.

The next morning, I wake up knowing that this will be the last day of our fishing trip. We start early, meeting for breakfast before sunrise. After the traditional toast and butter, I head out to the patio. The tiny hotel stands right on the edge of a lake with rolling hills behind. The rising sun sends purple and orange swatches of light across the lake. It is going to be a glorious day.

Or so I thought. The weather is perfect, in fact, and the stream is full of trout, but I am exhausted. I drag myself down the gorge after Lucas and find myself casting without much feeling. I am ready to head home, to see my babies, and to get some sleep. At about 11:00a.m., I tell Lucas that I've had about enough. He says that we should just hike a little further; there is one more pool we should explore.

A few minutes later, we are standing on the rocks, about twenty feet above the river. I look down and see that the stream is shaped like the number seven. It flows west to east, then takes a sharp bend south through some rapids and opens up into a large pool that is at least two hundred feet long. Looking down at the number 7 pool, I think about fishing beat number 7 on the Connetquot River and resting on the seventh day, Shabbat. Maybe this will be my lucky spot.

Lucas tells me to send the fly into the rapids right at the bend, and then let the black Woolly Bugger swing down. I cast down from the sky into the top of the pool. Nothing. Another cast yields the same result. It is definitely time to head home. I send the Woolly Bugger into the rapids and watch it swing around the bend. I pull up the rod to cast again, but this time it stops.

All of a sudden I hear the reel screeching as the line sails through it. I try to pull up the rod, but it won't move. Lucas turns to me and starts yelling, "Tension, tension. Don't lose the tension!" My heart is racing, adrenaline pumping. I've got something big on.

I try to reel in, but it is like trying to pull a tank through the water. Each time I manage to reel in a bit, the fish runs back down the pool. All I can think about is not pulling too hard and breaking the line. Finally, the trout crests and we see it. Lucas says "Whoa!" and my heart keeps pumping.

Each minute that I fight this behemoth of the river feels infinitely longer. Finally, I bring the trout to the net. Lucas estimates this fish as a twenty-two-inch five-pound female rainbow trout. I hold her in my arms and feel the weight of her body.

When Moses descended from Mount Sinai carrying the stone tablets with the Ten Commandments, the Bible says that he was radiant with divine revelation. Holding that five-pound rainbow in my hands, with a wide smile on my face, I feel as close to my own divine revelation as Moses had been.

We take a few pictures, and then Lucas says it's time to release her back into the stream. I lower my Goliath trout into the water and watch as she slowly descends back into the depths. I turn to Lucas, smile, and say "Thank you."

Lucas and I both take a deep breath, exhaling for what feels like the first time since I hooked the trout. He tells me he thought I was going to lose that fish for sure. He wants me to e-mail him a copy of that picture holding the trout, as this is the largest fish he has ever seen taken from the river.

We put down our fly rods and nets. Lucas fixes us both sandwiches of tuna fish on white bread with tomato. I have two. We talk about that trout and the fight to bring her to the net. We recap the trip. We smile and laugh, two trout bums sitting on a rock in the middle of Argentina, watching the river flow by.

A calm silence descends upon us, the silence of an adventure coming to an end. I feel gratitude wash over me like the cold waters of the stream. I give thanks for the miracle of a five-pound trout, growing healthy and strong in the river. I am grateful for Lucas, a kindred fishing soul, who brought me to this place. I look around, at the flowing river, at the rocks that line its shore, and up to the clear blue sky, and I give thanks to my Creator, the One who planted a garden of Eden in Argentina and let me come and visit.

I tell Lucas that it's time to go home, that there is no way we can possibly top catching that huge fish. As we walk back to the car, I realize that I may not see Lucas again for years, or make it back to the Rio

Quines. But this trip and that trout will forever live on in my memory and in my soul.

## Reflection Questions

1.  When have you traveled far from home to go fly-fishing, to seek adventure on a new river or stream? What other adventures have you pursued in life? When have you been afraid to go away from the familiar? How has that hampered you experiencing the fullness of life?

2.  When have you found yourself in a place where the people, culture, language, religious beliefs, or way of life were different? What did you learn from the experience? What did you discover in common with the place or the people?

3.  Whether in fly-fishing, our careers, or our relationships, it is easy to get stuck in a rut, to become overly comfortable with what we know. How open have you been to "new things" in your life? New ways of experiencing your time on the river? New ways of experiencing the spiritual side of existence?

4.  Where have there been *liminal* places in your life, thin places where the Divine and human come closer to connecting to one another? When have you had an experience on the trout stream or in nature that made you feel closer to a presence larger than yourself? Do you feel this same sort

of connection to the Divine in religious places like churches and synagogues? Why or why not?

5.  How have memories shaped your life? Has it been positively or negatively? Have you had a personal memory that functions as *anamnesis*—the bringing to life of something very powerful in your past that becomes a living reality in your daily life?

# Exercise: Keep a Fly-Fishing Travel Journal

- *Just write.* Starting a journal is always the hardest part. Where do I begin? What do I say? Who am I writing for? Just remember that some of the greatest journeys begin with challenges. Your journal shouldn't be formal or academic. It is a testimony written for your eyes only. No rules. No grades. No one looking over your shoulder. Just you and your words.

- *Observe.* Once you've arrived at your destination—whether your lodging location, the river where you will be fishing, or another leg of your journey—stop and take a moment to exercise all of your senses. Observe and record the sights, smells, and sounds all around you. Your journal doesn't have to outline each event of your day. Think about what's happening right now. Ask yourself questions. Who else is there? What are they doing? What conversations are you having?

What noises are you hearing? What is different about this place in contrast to others? What is the weather like and how is it impacting your mood that day? Pay attention to your surroundings and write down what happens. Anecdotes make for deeper stories.

- *Do it now.* Don't wait for inspiration; write whenever you have a moment to stop and pull out your journal. Traveling can be eventful and hectic at times. Make time for small moments of reflection. The stories will come.

- *Do it every day.* Writing in your journal on each day of your trip allows you to capture your thoughts while they are fresh. Impressions can be short-lived; get them down on paper before you lose them. Keeping up with your journal on a regular basis will provide a rich, meaningful account of your trip.

- *Gather souvenirs.* Collect and keep small mementos—such as rocks or a feather—that remind you of each part of your journey. If possible, use a journal that has pockets to make it easier to collect souvenirs. They will help transport you to a particular moment during your travels once you are back in home waters.

- *There are no rules.* Don't feel trapped by sentences or paragraphs. Make lists. Write single word impressions. Draw sketches. Write music lyrics.

Just put your pen or pencil on the page and let it flow.

- *Write about the unexpected.* All trips have surprises. Write about those unpredictable or bewildering experiences, too.

- *Ask your friends to contribute.* Travel companions may be on the same trip, but they have a unique perspective on the journey. New friends you meet along the way can bring new insights on events. Have them include their thoughts, questions, and observations in your journal, too.[1]

# CHAPTER SEVEN

# FLY-TYING

## A RECIPE FOR CREATIVITY

*I look into my fly box, and think about all the elements I should consider in choosing the perfect fly: water temperature, what stage of development the bugs are in, what the fish are eating right now. Then I remember what a guide told me: "90 percent of what a trout eats is brown and fuzzy and about five-eighths of an inch long."*

*—Allison Moir-Smith, angler, editor, and marriage guru*

# RABBI ERIC: STREAM AND SPIRIT

My fishing buddy Bob and I meet at the temple at 8:00p.m. on a Monday night. It's mid-December and it has already been dark for hours, since, this time of year, the sun sets in Connecticut at the depressing hour of 4:30. The parking lot is empty, except for our two cars. It is cold. The temple is deserted. Tonight, with Bob's help, I will be tying my first fly.

I suggest to Bob that we set up the fly-tying gear in the library. The temple is located in a renovated nineteenth century mansion, built originally by George

Doubleday, the chairman of the Ingersoll-Rand Company. The three-story wooden white mansion was his summer vacation home, as Ridgefield, Connecticut, is located only sixty miles from New York City.

The library was originally the mansion's living room. Then it served as the sanctuary where my congregation gathered on Friday nights to welcome the Sabbath and to pray together. Now we have a brand-new sanctuary farther down the hall, and the library is filled with volumes of Jewish history, literature, and sacred texts. A stone fireplace sits near the two sets of glass-paned double doors. As I walk into the room, I think about its history, from when it was a living room for George Doubleday, to a sanctuary, and finally to a library where Jewish wisdom is preserved and learned. Today it will be a place where a rabbi and his friend will be tying fishing flies.

I hear a rattle from the general direction of the fireplace. Bob smiles and says that it is the ghost of George Doubleday back to visit his old home. I double-check to see that the flue is closed, so that whatever is in the walls will stay there. A moment later the noise subsides, and we take out the fly-tying gear.

As Bob describes it, fly-tying is an art form. The painter begins with canvas and watercolors, dips the brush in the paint, and then uses delicate motions of the hands to bring a picture to life. With a knife and great skill, the wood carver transforms a log into an elegant wooden crane. The potter uses clay and, with the aid of a wheel and his or her hands, forms smooth vessels and vases. The art of tying a fly likewise blends the materials of nature, man-made tools, and precise movements to make a hook, thread, and feathers come to life as trout food.

Bob takes out two fly-tying vises. He will demonstrate each step, and I will repeat them. Every fly starts with a lone hook held in place by a fly-tying vise. Thread, wool, and feathers are wound, stretched, and secured to the hook by the bobbin, stacker, and hackle pliers. Portable lights and magnification aid the fly-tier in manipulating the tiny hooks and threads. Tools and materials come together in a series of movements honed over many hours spent at the fly-tying bench. Each technique has a name: the 45-degree roll, the pinch, tying off, and the whip finish. Gazing at the finished fly in the vise, the fly-tier realizes that he or she has performed a sort of miracle by bringing these raw materials to life, making thread, wool, and feathers look like a caddis fly about to land on the surface of the water.

Bob guides me through a dizzying series of steps to tie my first fly, an underwater nymph. I place a bead on the end of the hook to ensure that the fly will sink, and I secure the hook to the vice. I wind the brown thread around the hook. Some brown dubbing becomes the body. Next we use a gold thread and hackle pliers to imitate the segments of the insect. A bit of shimmering green dubbing goes near the bead.

Now, it's time for the whip finish. Bob holds out two fingers in the shape of a peace sign, makes some agile movements so that the thread becomes a triangle, weaves his fingers in and out a few times, and the fly is done. I have a feeling that the whip finish is going to whip me.

I show him the tool I bought that is supposed to make the whip finish easier, but that I do not know how to use. He's not sure either. Bob pulls out his phone and finds a YouTube video of someone at a fly shop in Montana demonstrating the proper use of the tool. I do my best, and a few moments later, I've tied my first fly. We apply some head cement to hold everything together, and the fly is done, a brown-and-green lifelike creation, ready for the trout stream.

As I stare at the finished fly in the vise, I ask Bob what kind of nymph we just tied. He calls it a Bob Special, as he made up the fly pattern himself based on the bugs he sees on the river.

The instructions for tying flies are called a pattern or a recipe. Following the directions as written will produce something that will appear tasty to a trout. But the most skilled fly-tiers, like the best chefs, find ways to go beyond the recipe. The innovation could be as simple as using a different color of thread or feather in a familiar fly pattern. Or it could involve tying something entirely new, like many famous anglers whose names are remembered in the flies they created: the Quill Gordon, named after one of the pioneers of American fly-fishing, Theodore Gordon; or the Royal Wulff, named after Lee Wulff and fished successfully by anglers for decades.

Creating something new from scratch, or tweaking the recipe, is also important in spiritual pursuits. The rabbis of the Talmud taught that Jewish prayer requires the interplay and balance of two fundamental elements: *keva,* the fixed words on the page, and *kavannah,* the intention of the worshipper. To focus only on the *keva,* reading and chanting the words each week by rote, may not lead to spiritually meaningful Jewish prayer. We must also bring ourselves into the words, praying with *kavannah,* intention, and offering the prayers with our hearts.

As I gaze at the Bob Special nymph that I just tied, I feel a sense of pride and accomplishment. I think about the creativity and artistry of turning a hook, thread, and feathers into a fly that a trout will see as a living being. With Bob's help, I have tried to channel my creative instincts and mimic our divine Creator. To form the first human being, Adam, God began with the dust of the earth, *adamah,* the raw materials. God then shaped the clay into a human form, using as tools the divine "hands." But God's greatest technique was yet to come, for a lump of clay is far from a human being. God blew into his nose *nishmat chaim,* the breath of life, and Adam became a living being. When tying flies, we, too, seek to breathe life, *nishmat chaim,* into our creations.

It took forty-five minutes to tie my first fly. I thank Bob for his help and patience. He is gracious as always. For the next hour we tie a few more Bob Specials, my skills improving with each wind of the thread over the hook and dubbing wound onto the thread.

Finally it is nearing 10:00p.m. and time to head home. The three Bob Specials that I tied are sitting on the table. I see the improvement in each one, as they became more proportioned and even. Then I realize that I did not bring a fly box to transport my new creations home. So I take off my blue fly-fishing hat, and I stick the three flies into the hard cloth of the hat, not too far from the large yellow *C.* I tell Bob that this is where they will stay for the rest of the winter. Then, one day in the not-too-distant future, when the earth wakes from her winter slumber, and the leaves return to the trees, and the bugs are buzzing, I'll tie on a Bob Special that I made with my own two hands, cast it into the stream, and hope that it will catch the eye of a large, lazy trout looking for an easy meal.

# REVEREND MIKE: FISHING INTO THE MYSTERY

Now we shift our focus to the practical yet beautiful things some of us do as anglers—tying our own flies. At times it is the first thing we may do before a trip, yet often it only comes after years of actual fishing.

In the Book of Common Prayer, a sacrament is defined as the "outward and visible sign of an inward and spiritual grace." In common understanding, a sacrament is nothing more than something that brings us into very intimate and close contact with God. It is the real tangible "stuff" of life. Traditionally, Christians have used sacramental language to describe events such as Baptism and Holy Communion. Water, wine, blood, bread—substances we are all familiar with.

Unfortunately, what is considered a sacrament was more or less defined by church officials—often to the detriment of our creativity and imagination. In the early 1970s, the Latin American liberation theologian, Leonardo Boff, wrote a book that turned this usage upside down. Called *Sacraments of Life: Life of the Sacraments,* the book made the bold claim that each of us can decide what the sacraments of our lives are. We know, Boff claimed, what brings us into the presence of God. The cover of the book had three bold images: a coffee cup, a loaf of bread, and a burning cigarette butt. For him, these three images represented—in their own way—images of childhood, his father, and the beginnings of his formation in faith. These things were, in fact, what brought him most intimately into the power and presence of holiness and the heart of the Divine.

We all have particular things that make us aware of the divine presence. For some, it is worship. For others, it may be prayer. For many, music fills that need. For many Christians, communion is something that they truly cannot live without. For Jews, the reading of the Torah scroll brings them closer to the Divine.

We all are wired differently, and I suspect that, as anglers, different parts of the fishing life set our souls free. We have touched on some of these topics in the preceding chapters. Yet for many, tying a fly represents a sort of final completeness, a moment of purity, an "outward and visible sign" of grace breaking into our lives. It symbolizes our beloved sport purely and, when done with reverence and imagination, it has the potential to serve as a sacramental act. It is often done in the darkness of the winter months, in the silence of a quiet room with a fire blazing and time for reflection and concentration.

For many anglers, tying their own flies is sort of an ethical process that makes their fishing experience more complete. I had fly-fished for forty years (a religious number, for sure, of "wandering and journey") before I tied my first fly a few years ago.

I had undergone major ankle surgery and was not able to ski one winter when I was at my Colorado home. I availed myself of this downtime to take fly-tying lessons, and found it to be one of the most profoundly spiritual disciplines I had ever experienced. It is almost a form of meditation, and once the nuances of finger and hand movements are learned, it is a journey to somewhere deep inside.

I often craft flies in the silence of my study, where I am surrounded by the clutter of books, icons, journals, not to mention the esoterica of fly-tying materials: multihued threads; natural furs and feathers; tiny, shimmering beads; flashing spools of wire; and hooks of various shapes and sizes. In my mind's eye, it is all transformed by alchemist's magic into something that is almost alive.

I imagine the flies darting and bobbing under the surface like a natural nymph, or floating and dancing on the top of the water in a perfect riffle, while the eyes of a hungry, wild trout home in on it before a savage strike. There is something so pure and wonderful about creating something that can make such a wild, focused creature as a trout think it is something floating downstream just for him.

I am not an "expert" in the technicalities of fly-tying, which is in and of itself an art form that takes decades to perfect. Yet, even in the absence of perfection, to catch a fish on an artificial fly that you tied yourself seems to be a morally good thing to do. Certainly it is more fulfilling at a deep emotional level than simply forking over $2 and buying one! It sort of equalizes the playing field, and funnels my total concentration and energy into the experience. Tying flies is a perfect way to spend a nice long winter evening, and is often enhanced by a fire in the background and beautiful music.

Like all inner journeys, the act and art of tying a beautiful fly finally takes us out into the world—the world of rivers, streams, and rising fish. Fly-fishing combined with the tying of a fly represents that critical intersection point between our inner journey and our outward ones.

## Reflection Questions

1. If you tie your own flies, describe how you first began and why you do it? If not, how can you get started?

2. Like the artistry in tying a fly, what are some parts of your life that required you to be creative? How can you bring more creativity into your days? When have you gone "beyond the recipe" in bringing something new into your life?

3. Tying flies is one way to stay connected to fly-fishing during the winter months. What are some other ways in which you use downtime that are meaningful and rewarding? When have you found unfilled and unscheduled time to be valuable?

## Exercise: Tie Your Own Fly

The best way to learn to tie fishing flies is with the help of a knowledgeable angler. Fly-fishing stores also sell basic fly-tying kits. The web is full of fly-tying websites with instructional videos. These basic instructions for tying a dry fly are from an article by outdoor writer and athletic coach Keith Dooley:[1]

**Basic Tools**

Fly-tying vise

Dry fly hook

Fly-tying thread

Thread bobbin

Animal hair, feathers, yarn

Scissors

**Basic Instructions**

1.  Place a dry fly hook in the jaws of the vise. Position the hook so that the vise jaws hold the bend of the hook in place with the shank on top and the point and barb on the bottom.

2.  Place a spool of fly-tying thread in a tying bobbin. Feed the thread through the thread guide in the bobbin and pull it out the front of the bobbin.

3.  Wrap the thread around the shank of the hook beginning just below the eye and working down to the bend. Wrap the thread back up to the eye and repeat the wrapping process two more times. This will build a base for adding fly-tying materials and begin to form a body for the fly.

4.  Add animal hairs, feathers, yarn, foam, and other materials in different combinations to imitate the shape and color of insects that might be on the

surface of the water. Tie animal hairs and feathers so they extend outward to imitate insect wings and provide buoyancy for the fly. Tie yarn in place on the shank of the hook with wide wraps of thread to allow the yarn fibers to show through, adding realism and interest to the fly.

5. Securely wrap the fly-tying thread around each layer of material. Make up to twenty turns of thread near the hook eye to finish the fly and create a head for it. Tie the thread off and cut it free with scissors. A simple double-overhand knot suffices for tying off the fly.

## CHAPTER EIGHT

# STEWARDSHIP AND CONSERVATION

### GIVING BACK TO THE STREAM

*We never know the worth of water till the well is dry.*

*—Dr. Thomas Fuller (1654–1734), English physician and writer*

## REVEREND MIKE: FISHING INTO THE MYSTERY

In the first chapter of Genesis, the writer describes the fifth and sixth days of creation as the times in which God made all the creatures of the earth followed by the creation of humankind in the divine image. Then in a startling and demanding image, God gives humans "dominion" over them all. In one fell swoop, creation and humanity are joined at the hip. Not separate. Not alone. But together, for better or worse. While scholars would argue that the translation of the original Hebrew and subsequent Latin word to "dominion" was a mistake, society has been plagued with it, nonetheless, for centuries.

There have been few words more abused and more misunderstood than *dominion.* It seems to imply dominance and control. It seems to imply both superiority and power, which as we all know can be utilized for both good and evil. The notion of dominion has been used to justify more possible types of exploitation of our planet and its resources than perhaps any other word or passage in the Bible. And yet we couldn't have been more confused about what this passage means as we listened to it in light of our love and concern for the waters we fish as anglers.

Not all of us have children, but for those who do, having children forces us to confront our own weaknesses, strengths, and responsibilities. In a very real way, for many years we have "dominion" over them. They are products of our love. Yet, we have incredible power over them both for good and for harm. When loved and nurtured, they grow to remarkable fruition as adults and beyond. We feed them, we clothe them, we mold and shape them, and, finally, we set them free. That is what love does. It is a caring, nurturing, tender mind-set that we bring to this immense responsibility of child rearing. Sometimes we do it well; other times we fail miserably. In a very real way, we could be said to have dominion over our children for the first few decades of their lives.

Yet in reality, all we really are are caretakers. We keep them healthy and protected in our love, and then we turn the rest of the journey over to God. We are stewards of our children, and that is a huge moral responsibility, not only for the nurture and sustenance of them, but also for the future of our planet. And so, our journeys as children, then adults, and now anglers have a common trajectory—we are caretakers of the gifts we are given. And the gifts of waters, wild places, and fish are among the many treasures of creation for many of us.

*Stewardship* is another daunting and misunderstood word. For many in church or religious life, it conjures images of an annual fund drive to meet the budget. It becomes crass, onerous, and a burden—instead of the joyous celebration of the many gifts we are given. But the meaning of the word is so nuanced that to reduce it to mere dollars and cents does not do it justice.

From a moral and theological perspective, it means we have ultimate personal responsibility for that to which we have been entrusted. So "giving back" to those things isn't some sort of mere duty or fiduciary responsibility. It is a way of saying that the things we believe in count for something, and that we are going to do our best to continue to nurture and care for those things—with our work, our resources, whatever they may be, and our actions. A gift was freely given, and now is much entrusted.

When all is said and done, this understanding leads to three components of any stance or action as it pertains to the environment. We can act morally, theologically, or practically. Some do one better than the others. Some integrate all three into the way they feel and behave. And unfortunately, some do none and slide through life living on the edges of responsibility—not necessarily out of malice but because of a lack of a certain perspective or accurate information.

In classical moral language, there are some things we are called to do because they are the "right things" to do. Kant would call this "duty" or the categorical imperative. Though Kant would argue against the attachment of emotional significance to this sense of duty, humans nonetheless experience the categorical imperative at a deeply emotional level. There are things we do with our lives simply because they speak to something in our inner beings. We recognize the "rightness" of them from the deepest parts of our soul. We know they make a difference. We know that our planet cannot forever sustain the continued onslaught it is now experiencing. Our hearts speak the truth, even when we are not prepared to hear it. From this perspective, responsible care for our waters is simply not something we can opt out of. We must do it, or be prepared to lose our treasure forever.

From a theological perspective, the Christian theologian Sallie McFague has pushed the envelope of environmental stewardship with a provocative book called *The Body of God: An Ecological Theology.* Bringing classical Christian terms into the discussion, she challenges us to rethink our understanding of the role we play in the created order. When we walk into our natural resources, we encounter nothing less than a holy, divine incarnation of a creating, loving God. It is not something we can abuse, take for granted, pillage or plunder, or otherwise use merely for our personal pleasure. Yes, we can all enjoy moments of pleasure on the rivers of our lives. Yes, we can have fun and let time there give us a brief respite from our daily cares and responsibilities. Yet all things gifted freely ultimately come with demands—of care, love, and sustenance.

In the gifts of wild places, we come to the stark reality that we are living in the most delicate and precarious of times. Between population growth, diminishing funds for protection of the environment, and an ever-more-acute need to "escape," our ecosystems are under siege. In the large scale, we are all too aware of the results of catastrophic environmental accidents. Yet it may be the accumulated damage of tiny daily things that otherwise caring, well-intentioned people do in their time in the wilderness that may do more long-term damage than the major publicized events. The adage "think globally, act locally" seems a perfect example of environmental stewardship that is both practical and immediate. If each of us picks up one beer can or piece of trash on a river every time we go there, the cumulative effect will have a far reaching impact.

It is all too easy to drift into nihilism or skepticism when faced with the magnitude of the issues of conservation and moral responsibility for our waters. In my home-waters watershed, the Roaring Fork Conservancy (www.roaringfork.org) is a wonderful example of how public-private partnerships can make a significant difference locally. example of how public-private partnerships can make a significant difference locally.

The conservancy focuses its educational and logistical out-reach on three areas of concern: water quantity, water quality, and habitat preservation. There are five related program areas: watershed education, land conservation, river stewardship, water-resources research, and water-quality monitoring. Over fifty government agencies have weighed in and participated in discussions that affect the water issues in our local watershed. School and adult educational programs have been developed where educators teach us all about "the ecological, chemical, physical, and cultural significance of local riparian areas using relevant, hands-on, place-based, interactive learning methods."

Whew! That's a mouthful. Yet when pared down to its basics, the whole premise is that the more we understand our watershed and its native species, the more we can take responsibility for its care. It is deeply meaningful when we can transform our beliefs from the merely theoretical into logistical and practical action. In a very real way, we move from our hearts to our heads and then to our bodies. Like the lessons we learn as children, we are finally called to a life of mature caring and love for something or someone beyond ourselves.

With all that in mind, let me take you to a river where dominion and stewardship clash on a grand scale that has been visible for decades to those of us who have fished there. The Pecos River outside of Santa Fe, New Mexico, is a lovely little Rocky Mountain river—full of both native and stocked trout, riffles and pools, multiple public access points, several nice feeder streams, and the magic light for which northern New Mexico is famous. The Pecos River is actually the home of the first native trout found in the New World—the Rocky Mountain cutthroat trout. But the river's very beauty, combined with easy accessibility, means that inevitable degradation is part of the story of the Pecos. The pressure it faces day in and day out—from locals, tourists, well-versed and responsible anglers, and greedy weekend visitors who view the river as their own personal fish market—has become a serious and ongoing problem.

I went up there one day to fish with my brother-in-law, David, and it took my breath away to witness the pillage of the beautiful river that I remembered from earlier years. Pull-out after pull-out was filled with campers, trash, crowds, and a general sensory overload. Beer cans were more plentiful than grass. In section after section on the river, daily limits were obviously being ignored. I was angry and ashamed of my fellow humans who had so little concern or reverence for where they were and what they were doing. It was nothing more than a free-for-all in the middle of one of the most historic fisheries in the West. I realized that in spite of our best efforts in the fishing community, we had failed in our responsibility to educate the public and change practices that are endemic to certain rivers and in certain parts of the country.

In contrast to that image, a few years later I was lucky enough to fish a private section of the Pecos. We got to cast in waters that had been developed and protected by guides, Trout Unlimited, and local volunteers who understood stream rehabilitation and conservation. The contrast between that section of the river and the others was painfully obvious. One was alive, healthy, and vibrant. The others were dying a slow death. I asked David, the best fly-fisher I know, how this could be so. How could we get to a point where good healthy waters are only available for a "select" few, and other identical waters are being lost by the day? We were both saddened by those realities, as we would love to see whole rivers become healthy enough to share, with others, the love of the sport we cherish. The stark realization is that unless we are able to educate and convince all parties that our rivers need not only our protection but our very love, the future for many rivers is not going to be pretty.

There are no easy answers to a set of circumstances that are often a combination of local issues, painful histories, and regulatory mechanisms that are misunderstood or frankly ignored. It is often not a question of right or wrong as much as "us" versus "them." Outsiders are seen as intruders into rights that go back centuries, and any notion of daily limits or conservation is simply not a part of the regional conversation. So, while many anglers have been raised in an era of environmental sensitivity and conservation, for many "locals" all over the country this sensitivity goes against deeply ingrained practices.

Often, coalitions of concerned citizens emerge who try to build bridges to local populations with very healthy results for river protection and conservation. Being a good Anglican, I tend to always seek the "via media" method—the middle way. I am very sensitive to cultural and historical traditions in which fishing was not only custom, but also an imperative for the sustenance of the family. These values and narrative elements are extremely important, and we should always factor those into current and future decisions and policy.

Yet I am also aware that resources are finite. They may be renewable, but they cannot sustain an exponential growth without permanent and non-repairable damage to the systems that birth them.

And so, when envisioning our future with our waterways and use of our watersheds, we should listen carefully and even prayerfully. We need our collective wisdom, input from all parties, and a brutal and frank discussion of what is at stake. For we are not only talking about small or regional issues, but the very health—moral, physical, and spiritual—of our planet.

In a very concrete way, we are heirs to what our ancestors, as well as those who were here before us, considered to be an "abundance" of natural resources. In fact, I do not feel it is hyperbole to claim that the North American continent was at one point a Western Hemisphere Eden, rich beyond measure in natural resources. And while it is too simplistic to say that it is now "desecrated," it would be obvious to all that the state of abundance is long diminished. Through both simple pressures of population growth and willful as well as unconscious acts, we are at a "tipping point" in our understanding of the wise and proper use of creation and its gifts.

In the Episcopal Book of Common Prayer we pray: "you made us fellow workers in your creation; give us wisdom and reverence so to use the resources of nature, that no one may suffer abuse of them, and that generations yet to come may continue to praise you for your bounty."

This lovely prayer captures in just a few short sentences the crux of the times we live in. We have not truly lived into the moral reality of being "fellow workers" in creation. And thus, we have slipped into a place and time in history where abundance is threatened. We are faced with the reality that unless practices and ethics are changed, future generations may not be able to praise God for this bounty we have been blessed with, for it will be gone, and we may not get many second chances. A vivid example of this is the current issue at play in the fight for Alaska's Bristol Bay fishery.

My nephew, Sam Snyder, is an avid fly-fisherman with a doctorate in environmental ethics and river conservation. He has been hired by a diverse group of coalitions in Alaska that are working to educate the public about a proposed mining project that could permanently eradicate the most productive sockeye-salmon fishery in the world. This fishery has provided sustenance for thousands of years to Alaska natives and now provides over 50 percent of the commercial sockeye salmon in the world, generates over $400 million in revenues, and employs over fifteen thousand people. In many respects, the fight to conserve Bristol Bay is the perfect example of the tension between "dominion" and "stewardship."

Writing from both a moral perspective and a religious sensibility, Sam feels that it is time for people of faith to "reconsider the role of their religion in this time of eco-crisis. Because many fly-fishers praise their tradition for the occasions it provides for them to connect to nature, they will contend these connections often lead them to be concerned about environmental degradation." In interviews Sam conducted, when asked if fly-fishing leads to paying attention to the "health" or "state" of the environment, one angler emotionally replied, "Well, of course. Being out there on a stream over the years, you notice changes from stream degradation to water loss." Another angler responded more broadly, "If you enjoy the environment in any way, you cannot help but support organizations and take care of it when you are out there."[1]

We all love to visit our wild places, to read about them, to treasure them in our hearts and souls. I know there are waters I shall never see or fish, yet the stories of them continue to enthrall me. I long for open spaces in which I seek my freedom and my God. They take me deep inside myself and challenge me to be a better and more loving person. Unless these places are carefully and fairly protected, I will never get the opportunity to take my grandchildren there and tell them stories from the banks of the water where the salmon run.

Making hard decisions is sometimes a moral imperative to ensure that future generations can know the joy and blessings we have been given. Sam understands this when he writes, "Even for those anglers who have never fished in Bristol Bay, the knowledge that places still exist where one can catch all five species of Pacific salmon and rainbow trout in their native waters, waters never impacted by hatcheries, and where there are more bears than people, carries with it a moral requirement to protect it."

For many, these discussions carry not only moral or philosophical weight, but are entirely driven by a theological perspective. We may come from various and diverse religious traditions, but time on the river carries us into a piece of the Divine that we all seem to share in common. We may use different terms to describe that part of the journey and different traditions to shape our responses to fish and water, but very few anglers are void of some sort of awareness that they are participating in something beyond themselves.

Again, Sam captures this reality: "Beyond statistics, however, fly-fishers around the world frequently describe their experiences of fishing through the use of terms such as religious, spiritual, sacred, divine, ritual, meditation, and conversion. Further, drawing upon religious terminology, fly-fishers will refer to rivers as their church and to nature as sacred. Often these latter pronouncements drive a concern for the conservation of said sacred spaces as evidenced by participation in local and national conservation organizations."

I would like to take that analogy one step further. If we can describe rivers as "sacred spaces" and time there as worship, then what we do there and beyond becomes a form of *liturgy*. Liturgy is simply the actions of our hands, voices, words, and songs that give life and meaning to worship. It is the physical and tangible expression of our shared faith. It is the skeleton upon which we graft the sinews of our very lives. Liturgy can be relaxed or formal, but, when done well, it always captures the essence of who we are as people of faith in any given religious tradition. So our words become not just empty phrases, but living realities that shape our collective consciousnesses and stories. It draws on the past as well as shapes the future.

In this sense, what we do in our time on the river, and in our lives that build on our river experiences, becomes a form of liturgy. When I pick up trash from a riverbank, I might say to myself the words we use upon offering the bread and wine at communion. "This is the Body of Christ, broken for you. This is the Blood of Christ, shed for you." These words, of course, then become more than just doctrine. They become a way of expressing the grief we experience when we recognize what we have done to our watersheds and our earth.

Yet these words are not only a source of the divine reality but an expression of the moral responsibility to heal wounds shared by all. They challenge us to find ways to protect our waters, nurture our fisheries, and sustain our planet for those that follow in our footsteps. To do anything else but live in the completeness of that responsibility is a breach of covenant that we have with our God as well as our fellow travelers.

But we must be mindful of the deep chasm between "contract" and "covenant." In my coauthor's and my shared religious traditions, a covenant emerged between God and his chosen people, which was then extended to "all the peoples of the earth." It was a divine promise that God will be with us, and it has become a living template for a holy, mutually obligatory relationship. It is not a legal contract. It is not a static, dry document that binds us to a distant past. It is a living, breathing awareness that our ongoing relationship with God is dynamic, fluid, and intimate. It is a promise from both parties that we will always be faithful.

In this sense, covenants are alive. They shape and mold the marrow of our lives and guide us to a shared destiny. Like it or not, we are joined together on this living planet. Our lives and our destinies are intertwined, and our health and the healing of our planet and waters are one and the same. When we nurture, care for, and protect our waters, we are truly alive in a beautiful and eternal expression of covenant that we keep not out of duty alone, but out of love for what we have been given. The choice is ours to make, and how well we choose shapes our common lives both during our time here and the time to come.

# RABBI ERIC: STREAM AND SPIRIT

The alarm clock rang at 4:45a.m., well before the first light of dawn. I was twenty years old, home in

St. Louis for the summer from Tufts University in Boston, and I was headed to my first trout stream.

Two weeks previously I had seen *A River Runs Through It* at the Hi-Pointe Theatre, and was immediately hooked on fly-fishing. I found my way to the local fly shop on Manchester Boulevard and purchased my St. Croix fly rod, rubber hip boots, leaders, and flies. I spent a few days teaching myself to cast on the front lawn, wisely, without a hook, as the line came perilously close to my face numerous times. Finally I felt ready to cast on the stream for the first time, and who knows, maybe even tempt a trout to rise.

I was so excited I barely slept that August night. I headed out the door at 5:00a.m. Fishing starts early in Missouri, and the trout park where I was headed opened at 6:00. Of course I wanted to be there for the first cast.

It was already hot out, and I knew it would be another sweltering day. For the next hour, I drove from city to interstate to rural roads. The sun began to peek above the horizon, bringing light to the scattered barns and wheat fields that stretched into the distance. I wound through the curves, alone on the road, the warm air flowing through the open windows of my car.

At the state park I headed to the bait shop where, for once, I did not purchase bait but picked up a trout tag and a map of the river. I put together my rod and prepared my gear. I sat in the car for a few minutes, ate my bagel, and waited. At 6:00a.m. sharp, the siren blared, indicating that the stream was open. I abandoned the rest of my breakfast, grabbed my rod, and headed to the stream.

I staked out the most popular part of the river, figuring that, as a beginner, I would have my best shot at catching a trout there. I walked with a half dozen other anglers, all of whom were using spin rods and bait. We wished each other good morning and good luck. As usual, I appreciated the midwestern kindness that I grew up with.

As I approached the stream to cast a fly for the first time, I saw images from *A River Runs Through It* and its Montana rivers in my head. I was ready to wade into the cold water, to cast to the wily trout, to soak in the beauty of the river. I was excited. I was ready to be inspired.

I stopped at the stream's edge. The water was so clear that I could see right down to the riverbed, which was covered with fish carcasses. They were everywhere, literally dozens of them, all trout that had been cleaned and skinned and left in the water like trash.

I stood there for a moment, shocked. I asked a fellow angler next to me, a tall man with a trimmed brown beard, what was going on. He said that anglers were allowed to keep five trout a day from this river. Rather than clean their fish at home or in the woods, some of our fellow anglers chose to use the cold water to prepare their trout fillets and just discard the leftover fish carcasses right there in the river. We both shook our heads in dismay. Before I had even cast my first fly to a trout, I realized that the rivers and streams of our world are fragile, precious, and need our protection.

I left the fish graveyard and began to follow the map and my feet along the river, away from the parking lot and the other anglers. I saw a tiny creek that fed into the stream. Following the flowing water a few hundred feet through the woods, I discovered the creek's source, a clear spring pool.

At every moment, cold pure water pulsed from the earth to fill this pool that fed the river below. I paused and gave thanks for this miracle of nature, for the life-giving water that flowed out of the ground to sustain the trout, the bugs, and all living things.

As I stared into the spring, I saw movement. There were trout there, too, swimming in the depths of the pool, enjoying the pure water.

I finally took my first, official cast with a fly rod. It was not graceful, nor were the half dozen that followed. But somehow I managed to land my dry fly on the pool's surface, not too far from the trout swimming below. I watched in amazement as a single fish broke ranks with its compatriots, swam up quickly toward the surface, and grabbed my fly with a tiny splash.

I jerked the rod up in my excitement, just like I used to do when I fished for bass with my dad at Busch's Wildlife only a hundred miles or so away from where I stood. Miraculously, I did not break the line, and I shortly reeled in my first trout, an eight-inch rainbow. In my elation, it felt more like eighty inches. I smiled in amazement at being able to hold such a beautiful creature in my hands.

As I looked at the small trout, I thought of all of the fish remains that were scattered downstream. I could not do that to this fish, a fellow living creature, one of God's creations. I managed to get the hook out of the trout's mouth without causing it too much harm and returned it to the river. The fish dove deep into the pool, and I felt at peace.

On my first fly-fishing trip ever, I caught a small trout. But I also learned that the fish and the rivers need our help if they are to survive and flourish. Between the spring and the fish graveyard, I saw the pristine beauty of undisturbed nature, and I saw how we can harm and even destroy those gifts.

In the years since that morning on a Missouri stream, my fly-fishing skills have grown. So, too, has my concern for, and involvement in, protecting the places that trout call home. For me, the two go hand in hand.

When I am out on the river, I take small steps to help the earth. I pick up trash and stuff it into my waders to throw away later. I figure I am dirty already; what's the harm in adding a few extra plastic wrappers or empty beer cans?

Along with tens of thousands of other anglers, I am a member of Trout Unlimited, a nonprofit organization that works to protect rivers and watersheds. Each of the hundreds of local chapters, including my own Candlewood Valley group in Connecticut, perform stream cleanup, seek to educate others about river conservation issues, and get together to talk trout, flies, and all things fishing.

While on the river, I practice catch-and-release, keeping a trout only where regulations allow. Trout are a finite resource, and if we kept every fish that we caught, the streams would soon be empty. I return trout to their streams so that other anglers, and someday my children and grandchildren, will be able to fish these rivers and streams and find the small thrill that I do when the line goes taut.

Like the spring-fed Missouri stream where I cast my first fly, the Garden of Eden was watered by a great river that sustained plants, trees, and the first human beings. I'd like to believe that this primeval river was filled with trout and that Adam and Eve might have cast a fly there.

God placed the first human beings in the Garden to "till it and to tend it." We must use the land wisely to ensure that it will flourish for all the generations to come. The Hebrew word for "to tend," *shamar*, also means "to protect." A *shomer* is a guard. As anglers who have the privilege of holding a trout in our hands, we are guardians of the streams, the rivers, and all of the natural places that make up our beautiful world.

## Reflection Questions

1.  How can the experience of casting a fly and wading into the river lead the angler to be concerned for the stream and our larger environment? When have you experienced a river that has been ruined by human overuse?

2.  What steps have you taken as an angler to protect the streams and rivers where you fish? How have you shared your concern for protecting the trout streams with others?

3.  How would God want us to treat the rivers, the streams, and the trout that live in them? What role can religion play in motivating people to help protect the planet?

## Exercise: Get Involved to Protect the Rivers You Fish

Conservation of rivers and streams is the primary mission of Trout Unlimited (www.tu.org) and the Federation of Fly Fishers (www.fedflyfishers.org). We are both proud members of TU and FFF and participate in our local chapters.

To begin to take steps toward protecting the streams you fish, consider taking the following conservation pledge from Recycled Fish:

- I pledge to live a lifestyle of stewardship on and off the water. Living as a steward means making choices throughout my daily life that benefit lakes, streams, and seas—and the fish that swim in them—because my *lifestyle runs downstream.*

- I will learn the fish and game laws where I hunt or fish and always abide by them.

- I will practice "catch and release" and "selective harvest" faithfully and responsibly.

- I will "police my resource" by turning in poachers and reporting polluters.

- I will make up for "the other guy" by cleaning up litter wherever my adventures take me.

- I will boat safely and responsibly, never trespass, and treat other enthusiasts respectfully.

- I will provide my time, money, or other resources to support stewardship efforts.

- I will take steps to see that my home, lawn, vehicle, workplace, and everyday lifestyle are as fish-friendly as I can make them by reducing my water, energy, material, and chemical footprint.

- I will encourage others to take on this ethic and will connect others with the outdoors to grow the stewardship community.

- I choose to serve as a role model in protecting what remains and recovering what's been lost of our wild and natural places.

- I am a steward.[2]

# ACKNOWLEDGMENTS

## RABBI ERIC'S ACKNOWLEDGMENTS

This book is the culmination of years spent standing in cold-water streams, listening to water flow over rocks, watching sunsets, and holding the occasional trout in hand. Bringing my angling experiences to life in this book would not have been possible without our incredible editor and fishing buddy, Kim Kafka—also known as "K2"—who slaved over this project and to whom I owe an eternal debt of thanks. I am also grateful to the wonderful editors and staff at SkyLight Paths; Emily Wichland, vice president of Editorial and Production; Justine Earnest, assistant editor; and Stuart M. Matlins, publisher. Thank you for continuing to publish books that explore the spiritual potential inherent in every aspect of life.

From the streams of Connecticut and New York, I offer my thanks to my friends Kenneth Lokensgard (the fly-fishing professor), Aron Hirt-Manheimer, and Jason Kaufman, who all helped to shape this book. I wish to thank my wife, Marcela, who read over countless drafts of the manuscript and who occasionally lets me escape to the river while holding down the fort at home; you make every part of my life possible. And, lastly, to my twins, my little boy and girl, Jonah and Naomi: this book is dedicated to you, for in a few years we will head to the stream together to cast our flies in search of trout and something more.

# REVEREND MIKE'S ACKNOWLEDGMENTS

There are so many who have shaped my life and experience over the last forty years, and as a result, have contributed to the creation of this book in many ways. I give thanks to David Snyder—my brother-in-law, my best friend, my fishing companion, my writing mentor, and my deepest colleague in every level of my being. You are the best angler I have ever seen, bar none. We have shared everything—medicine, broken patients that broke our hearts, fishing trips that led us to still waters and the restoration of our souls, and a life well-traveled together, full of family and ties that bind. Without your example, I would not have reached this level of love or passion for our shared sport. You are everything I aspire to be—as a man and as an angler. For my wife, Gail, who puts up with my obsessions and surely time consuming addictions. You are the blessing of my life. To my friends in Colorado—the wonderful staff at Taylor Creek Fly Shop and to JL, the head fishing guide at the Roaring Fork Club. Their love of the sport, their generosity of spirit, their knowledge they so freely share, and their long history of kindness to the stranger embodies everything that is wonderful about the sacred art of fly-fishing.

I offer special thanks to Kim Kafka, our content editor. As I write these words, we still have not met face to face nor have we fished side by side. Kim—for reasons that elude me—has seen into my deepest parts. She knows my strengths as a writer as well as my weaknesses. She sees me as I am, not as I wish I were. She knew when to lavish praise and when to crack the whip. She had mercy on my often ridiculous schedule and had the patience of a saint when putting up with my tendency to procrastinate. She has some sort of strange, even mystical sense with words—how they can shape, mold, and move us, and their ability to express something transcendental. She has begun the difficult task of teaching me how to grow as a writer, and if I have fallen short it is due to my own issues and not her lack of passion or talents. She "sees me"—perhaps the greatest gift of understanding one human can give to another.

I have often described the art of writing a bit like riding naked in a school bus. I suppose at some level we all fear being seen in a raw, pure state. Perhaps it is a fear of being unloved and unappreciated—although there may be more to it than that. Sharing these words has taught me something about myself as well as my friends and colleagues on this journey. This book is dedicated to those precious few, friends one and all.

# NOTES

## CHAPTER 2

[1]   Exercise taken from *A Wild Faith: Jewish Ways into Wilderness, Wilderness Ways into Judaism* by Mike Comins (Woodstock, VT: Jewish Lights Publishing, 2007).

## CHAPTER 3

[1]   Merton, Thomas. Edited by Jonathan Montaldo, *Dialogues with Silence: Prayers & Drawings* (New York: HarperOne, 2004).

[2]   See www.ehow.com/how_16390_basic-cast-fly.html.

[3]   See www.springcreekanglers.com/castingcoach_leftyprinciples.htm.

## CHAPTER 4

[1]   Adapted from the Personal Excellence blog by Celestine Chua.

## CHAPTER 6

[1]   Exercise adapted from "How to Keep a Travel Journal—Tips for Writing on the Road" by Pam Bauer (Los Angeles: *Road & Travel magazine,*

2007). see www.roadandtravel.com/traveladvice/2007/travel-journal-writing.htm.travel-journal-writing.htm.

# CHAPTER 7

[1]   See Keith Dooley's instructions at www.ehow.com/print/how_6695870_fly_tying-instructions.html, accessed 2/28/2011.

# CHAPTER 8

[1]   *Journal of the American Academy of Religion.* Journal published quarterly by Oxford University Press. Also available at http://jaar.oxfordjournals.org/.

[2]   See www.recycledfish.org/lifestyle-of-stewardship/sportsmans-stewardship-pledge.htm.sportsmans-stewardship-pledge.htm.

# SUGGESTIONS FOR FURTHER READING

## FLY-FISHING

Rosenbauer, Tom. *The Orvis Fly-Fishing Guide, Completely Revised and Updated.* Guilford, CT: Lyons Press, 2007.

Lord, Macauley, Dick Talleur, and Dave Whitlock. *The L.L. Bean Ultimate Book of Fly Fishing.* Guilford, CT: Lyons Press, 2006.

Santella, Chris. *Fifty Places to Fly Fish Before You Die.* New York: Stewart, Tabori and Chang, 2004.

Maclean, Norman. *A River Runs Through It and Other Stories.* 25th anniv. ed. Chicago: University of Chicago Press, 2001.

Prosek, James. *Fly-Fishing the 41st, From Connecticut to Mongolia and Home Again: A Fisherman's Odyssey.* New York: HarperCollins Publishers, 2003.

Duncan, David James. *The River Why.* 20th anniv. ed. San Francisco: Sierra Club Books, 2002.

Gierach, John. *Death, Taxes and Leaky Waders: A John Gierach Fly-Fishing Treasury.* New York: Simon & Schuster, 2001.

# SPIRITUALITY

Buber, Martin. *I and Thou.* trans. Ronald Gregor Smith, New York: Scribner, 2000.

Heschel, Abraham Joshua. *The Sabbath.* New York: Farrar Straus Giroux, 2005.

Kushner, Lawrence. *God Was in This Place & I, i Did Not Know: Finding Self, Spirituality, and Ultimate Meaning.* Woodstock, VT: Jewish Lights Publishing, 1993.

Jones, Tony. *The Sacred Way: Spiritual Practices for Everyday Life.* Grand Rapids: Zondervan, 2005.

Holt, Bradley P. *Thirsty for God: A Brief History of Christian Spirituality.* 2nd ed. Minneapolis: Fortress Press, 2005.

Lionberger, John. *Renewal in the Wilderness: A Spiritual Guide to Connecting with God in the Natural World.* Woodstock, VT: SkyLight Paths, 2007.

McFague, Sallie. *The Body of God: An Ecological Theology.* Minneapolis: Augsburg Fortress, 1993.

Merton, Thomas. *Contemplation in a World of Action.* Notre Dame, IN: University of Notre Dame Press, 1999.

# FLY-FISHING RESOURCES

The resources listed below are not intended to be comprehensive but rather a snapshot of the organizations out there that can help you get started or more involved in fly-fishing. Each description is taken directly from the organization's website.

# NATIONAL ORGANIZATIONS

## Trout Unlimited

www.tu.org
1300 N. 17th St.
Suite 500
Arlington, VA 22209-2404
800-834-2419

"Since 1959, Trout Unlimited has worked to conserve, protect and restore North America's coldwater fisheries and their watersheds." Local chapters meet throughout the country.

## Federation of Fly Fishers

www.fedflyfishers.org
Federation of Fly Fishers Museum
5237 US HWY 89 S, Suite 11
Livingston, MT 59047
406-222-9369

"Dedicated to Conserving, Restoring, and Educating through Fly Fishing." Local chapters meet throughout the country.

## Casting for Recovery
www.castingforrecovery.org
P.O. Box 1123
3738 Main Street
Manchester, VT 05254
802-362-9181

"Provides fly-fishing retreats specifically tailored for women who have or have had breast cancer."

## Reel Recovery
www.reelrecovery.org
160 Brookside Road
Needham, MA 02492
800-699-4490

"A national non-profit organization that conducts free fly-fishing retreats for men recovering from all forms of cancer."

# LOCAL ORGANIZATIONS

# *WESTERN UNITED STATES*

## Roaring Fork Conservancy
www.roaringfork.org
P.O. Box 3349
Basalt, CO 81621

970-927-1290

"Inspiring people to explore, value, and protect the Roaring Fork Watershed."

**Henry's Fork Foundation**
www.henrysfork.org
P.O. Box 550
606 Main Street
Ashton, ID 83420
208-652-3567

"An organization founded twenty-five years ago to protect the unique fishery, wildlife, and aesthetic qualities of the Henry's Fork watershed, and is the only conservation organization exclusively focused on this critical landscape."

**Northwest Fly Anglers**
www.northwestflyanglers.org
P.O. Box 75212
Seattle, WA 98175

"Dedicated to education, service, conservation and support while pursuing the art of angling with a fly."

**California Fly Fishers Unlimited (CFFU)**
www.cffu.org
P.O. Box 162997
Sacramento, CA 95816

"Dedicated to promoting awareness and participation in the art of fly fishing and promoting the conservation, preservation, and enhancement of our fishery resources."

## *NORTHEAST*

**The New England Fly Tyers (NEFT)**
www.newenglandflytyers.org
P.O. Box 164
Worceser, MA 01613

"A non-profit organization of fly fishers and fly tyers, fostering the art of fly tying, promoting the challenge of fly fishing, and encouraging conservation and sportsmanship."

**The American Museum of Fly Fishing**
www.amff.com
4104 Main Street
Manchester, VT 05254
802-362-3300

"Dedicated to preserving & exhibiting the treasures of American angling."

**Catskill Fly Fishing Center and Museum**
www.cffcm.net
1031 Old Route 17
Livingston Manor, NY 12758
845-439-4810

"A non-profit, educational organization dedicated to: preserving America's fly-fishing heritage; teaching its future generations of flyfishers; and protecting its fly-fishing environment."

## Theodore Gordon Flyfishers
www.theodoregordonflyfishers.org
P.O. Box 2345
Grand Central Station
New York, NY 10163

"A not-for-profit angling organization, founded on American fly-fishing traditions, promoting stream and river protection and self-sustainable salmonid populations through conservation, environmental oversight, activism, catch-and-release practices, and education."

## Long Island Flyrodders
www.liflyrodders.org
P.O. Box 8091
Hicksville, NY 11802

"Born in 1981 by a handful of dedicated fly fisherman from Long Island and Queens. It is a club dedicated to the sport of fly fishing."

# MIDWEST

## Michigan Fly Fishing Club (MFFC)
www.mffc.org
P.O. Box 530861
Livonia, MI 48153

"For more than thirty years the MFFC has been southeast Michigan's premier organization for fly fishing enthusiasts and introducing newcomers to this amazing pastime."

## Badger Fly Fishers
www.badgerflyfishers.org
N7111 County Road CC
Monticello, WI 53570-9586

## DRiFT—DuPage Rivers Fly Tyers
www.driftorg.com
P.O. Box 5028
Wheaton, IL 60189

"Aiming to preserve, protect, and enhance to its fullest potential the fresh and salt water fisheries for present and future generations of fly fishers, as well as publicize the best practices and techniques of fly fishing, fly tying, casting, and other related subjects."

# SOUTH

## Florida Fly Fishing Association
www.floridafly-fishing.org
P.O. Box 542345
Merrit Island, FL 32954

"Dedicated to the knowledge, fellowship, and enjoyment of fly fishing as well as the protection and conservation of Florida's fisheries."

**Atlanta Fly Fishing Club**
www.atlantaflyfishingclub.org
3 Brookhollow Road SW
Rome, GA 30165

"Organized in 1990 by a small group of fly fishermen with people like you in mind. Its goals continue to focus on promoting the sport of fly fishing through educational and other awareness programs in this region."

# CANADA

**British Columbia Federation of Fly Fishers (BCFFF)**
www.bcfff.bc.ca
P.O. Box 43
Vernon, B.C. V1T 6M1

"A registered, non-profit society whose main objective is to promote the conservation of the fishing environment in British Columbia."

**Izaak Walton Fly Fishing Club**
www.iwffc.ca
2400 Dundas Street West, Unit, Suite 283
Mississauga, Ontario L5K 2R8
905-279-6345

"A public, non-profit group of men, women and youth who enjoy fly fishing. The club was formed in February

1971 to promote fly fishing and conservation of our aquatic resources."

# BLOGS, WEBSITES, AND FORUMS

**The Fly Fishing Rabbi**
www.flyfishingrabbi.com
Written by coauthor Rabbi Eric Eisenkramer

"A Blog about Trout, God, and Religion"

**Fishing for History**
www.fishinghistory.blogspot.com

"The History of Fishing and Fishing Tackle"

**The Trout Underground**
www.troutunderground.com

"Fly Fishing's Fun, Independent Site"

**Moldy Chum**
www.moldychum.com

"Blog, Photos, Podcasts, Travel, Gear, and More"

**She Loves to Fish**
www.shelovestofish.com

"She was introduced to fishing at five years old and has been hooked ever since."

**FlyFisherGirl.com**
www.flyfishergirl.com

"Real Women, Real Fish, Real Adventure"

**The North American Fly Fishing Forum**
www.theflyfishingforum.com

**North Eastern Fly Fishing Forum**
www.njflyfishing.com

**Southeast Fly Fishing Forum**
www.southeastflyfishingforum.com

**Washington Fly Fishing Forum**
www.washingtonflyfishing.com

**Classic Fly Rod Forum**
www.clarksclassicflyrodforum.yuku.com

# *Spiritual Practice*

**Fly-Fishing—The Sacred Art:** Casting a Fly as a Spiritual Practice
*by Rabbi Eric Eisenkramer and Rev. Michael Attas, MD; Foreword by Chris Wood, CEO, Trout Unlimited; Preface by Lori Simon, executive director, Casting for Recovery*
Shares what fly-fishing can teach you about reflection, awe and wonder; the benefits of solitude; the blessing of community and the search for the Divine.

*Lectio Divina*—**The Sacred Art:** Transforming Words & Images into Heart-Centered Prayer  *by Christine Valters Paintner, PhD*
Expands the practice of sacred reading beyond scriptural texts and makes it accessible in contemporary life.

**Haiku—The Sacred Art:** A Spiritual Practice in Three Lines
*by Margaret D. McGee*

**Dance—The Sacred Art:** The Joy of Movement as a Spiritual Practice
*by Cynthia Winton-Henry*

**Spiritual Adventures in the Snow:** Skiing & Snowboarding as Renewal for Your Soul
*by Dr. Marcia McFee and Rev. Karen Foster; Foreword by Paul Arthur*

**Divining the Body:** Reclaim the Holiness of Your Physical Self  *by Jan Phillips*

**Everyday Herbs in Spiritual Life:** A Guide to Many Practices
*by Michael J. Caduto; Foreword by Rosemary Gladstar*

**Giving—The Sacred Art:** Creating a Lifestyle of Generosity
*by Lauren Tyler Wright*

**Hospitality—The Sacred Art:** Discovering the Hidden Spiritual Power of Invitation and Welcome  *by Rev. Nanette Sawyer; Foreword by Rev. Dirk Ficca*

**Labyrinths from the Outside In:** Walking to Spiritual Insight—A Beginner's Guide
*by Donna Schaper and Carole Ann Camp*

**Practicing the Sacred Art of Listening:** A Guide to Enrich Your Relationships and Kindle Your Spiritual Life  *by Kay Lindahl*

**Recovery—The Sacred Art:** The Twelve Steps as Spiritual Practice  *by Rami Shapiro; Foreword by Joan Borysenko, PhD*

**Running—The Sacred Art:** Preparing to Practice  *by Dr. Warren A. Kay; Foreword by Kristin Armstrong*

**The Sacred Art of Chant:** Preparing to Practice
*by Ana Hernández*

**The Sacred Art of Fasting:** Preparing to Practice
*by Thomas Ryan, CSP*

**The Sacred Art of Forgiveness:** Forgiving Ourselves and Others through God's Grace
*by Marcia Ford*

**The Sacred Art of Listening:** Forty Reflections for Cultivating a Spiritual Practice
*by Kay Lindahl; Illus. by Amy Schnapper*

**The Sacred Art of Lovingkindness:** Preparing to Practice
*by Rabbi Rami Shapiro; Foreword by Marcia Ford*

**Sacred Attention:** A Spiritual Practice for Finding God in the Moment
*by Margaret D. McGee*

**Soul Fire:** Accessing Your Creativity
*by Thomas Ryan, CSP*

**Thanking & Blessing—The Sacred Art:** Spiritual Vitality through Gratefulness
*by Jay Marshall, PhD; Foreword by Philip Gulley*

184

# BACK COVER MATERIAL

## Discover the spiritual potential hidden in every cast of the fly rod

"For us, fly-fishing is about more than catching fish. We have been skunked on the stream too many times to count, and stood shivering in our waders in 45-degree water long after sundown. Yet, every chance we get, we head back to the river in search of trout and something more."

### —from Rabbi Eric's Introduction

"Early in my fly-fishing career I remember telling a friend that there is so much to learn! Some forty years later, that is still true. Every trip I learn something new about rivers, fish and the natural world. Most importantly, I learn something new about myself. Every encounter with the waters of our planet draws me deeper into who I am and who I want to become."

### —from Reverend Mike's Introduction

In this unique exploration of fly-fishing as a spiritual practice, an Episcopal priest and a rabbi share what fly-fishing has to teach us about reflection, awe and the wonder of the natural world, the benefits of solitude, the blessing of community and the search for the Divine. Tapping the wisdom in the Christian and Jewish traditions and their own geographically diverse experiences on the water, they show how time spent on the stream can help you navigate the currents and eddies of your own inner journey.

"Offers beautiful and original perspectives on a pastime that for many is a kind of religion. They find common ground in the rivers they fish and the spiritual truths they encounter. Lovely, learned, personal, heartwarming and instructional."

—**JAMES PROSEK,** *author, Trout: An Illustrated History* and *Fly-Fishing the 41st: From Connecticut to Mongolia and Home Again—A Fisherman's Odyssey*

"Tastefully integrates valuable fly-fishing principles, accounts of adventures and deep spiritual truths that we can all apply to our lives and reflect on when we are on the water."

—**ITALO LABIGNAN,** television host, Canadian Sportfishing

"Clearly [shows] we are all united in our spirit.... A great read for anyone who cares about people, the conservation of our planet or learning to fly-fish."

—**SHERRY STEELE,** communications chair, Federation of Fly Fishers National Board of Directors

Made in the USA
Middletown, DE
27 August 2019